Daring to Share

*Multi-Denominational Congregations
in the United States and Canada*

SANDRA BEARDSALL
MITZI J. BUDDE
WILLIAM P. MCDONALD

PICKWICK *Publications* · Eugene, Oregon

DARING TO SHARE
Multi-Denominational Congregations in the United States and Canada

Copyright @2018 Sandra Beardsall, Mitzi J. Budde, William P. McDonald. All rights reserved. Except for brief quotations in critical publications or reviews, no part of this book may be reproduced in any manner without prior written permission from the publisher. Write: Permissions, Wipf and Stock Publishers, 199 W. 8th Ave., Suite 3, Eugene, OR 97401.

Scripture quotations are from New Revised Standard Version Bible, copyright © 1989 National Council of the Churches of Christ in the United States of America. Used by permission. All rights reserved worldwide.

Pickwick Publications
An Imprint of Wipf and Stock Publishers
199 West 8th Avenue, Suite 3
Eugene, Oregon 97401

www.wipfandstock.com

PAPERBACK ISBN: 978-1-5326-3913-5
HARDCOVER ISBN: 978-1-5326-3914-2
EBOOK ISBN: 978-1-5326-3915-9

Cataloging-in-Publication data:

Names: Beardsall, Sandra. | Budde, Mitzi J. | McDonald, William P.

Title: Daring to share : multi-denominational congregations in the United States and Canada / by Sandra Beardsall, Mitzi J. Budde, and William P. McDonald.

Description: Eugene, OR : Pickwick Publications, 2018 | Includes bibliographical references.

Identifiers: ISBN 978-1-5326-3913-5 (paperback) | ISBN 978-1-5326-3914-2 (hardcover) | ISBN 978-1-5326-3915-9 (ebook)

Subjects: LCSH: Churches—United States. | Churches—Canada.

Classification: LCC BV700 D18 2018 (print) | LCC BV700 (ebook)

Manufactured in the U.S.A.   06/27/18

For our spouses: Bill, John, and Carolyn
and
for all those who share the Gospel across boundaries day by day.

As Christians experience lifelong growth into Christ,
they will find themselves growing closer to one another.

—*The Church: Towards a Common Vision*

Contents

Acknowledgments | ix

Introduction | 1

A Note on Research Methodology | 7

Part I: Models

1 Full Communion Parishes | 13

2 Two Traditions Forging Partnership | 27

3 Crossing the Protestant-Roman Catholic Boundary | 40

4 Multiple Denominational Affiliations | 54

5 The Long Generation | 66

Part II: Living Into Shared Ministry Partnerships

6 Parish Life Cycles and Multi-Denominational Ministries | 85

7 "They Turned to Face Us" Worshiping Together | 97

8 The Gift(?) of Governance | 111

9 Maintaining Good Judicatory Relations | 125

Part III: Futures

10 Formation for Service in a Multi-Denominational Congregation | 137

11 Do You Have to Be Something? Multiple Belonging | 146

12 Keeping the Faith: Ecclesiology | 154

Bibliography | 171

Acknowledgments

We three authors of *Daring to Share* are colleagues who first met at annual gatherings of the North American Academy of Ecumenists, where we discovered a common desire to research and write about multi-denominational congregations. We wish to thank the many persons and institutions that helped our project come to fruition.

We owe a great debt of gratitude to all those who allowed us to invite ourselves into their multi-denominational congregations. Our interviewees generously welcomed us into their parishes, homes, and lives, and freely offered their candid and heartfelt experiences with us. Their insights helped bring the story to life. Students at the Saskatoon Theological Union and Virginia Theological Seminary offered lively contributions to the project.

The Saskatoon Theological Union oversaw our research ethics protocol. Virginia Theological Seminary generously funded an authors' meeting in Alexandria. Each of us is grateful for the financial grants that funded our travel to congregations and archival collections. Sandra received the McGeachy Senior Scholarship of the United Church of Canada; Mitzi received a Conant Grant from the Episcopal Church; and William received the Appalachian College Association Fellowship.

We stand on the shoulders of visionaries who pioneered and helped to foster shared congregations, including the Rev. Harvie Barker, who edited a compilation of Canadian shared ministry stories and continued to assist us in any way he could. Archivists across Canada provided valuable assistance, particularly Blair Galston of the British Columbia Conference Archives in Vancouver. Cheryl and Bruce Harding offered their home and hospitality to Sandra during her Vancouver stay. Robert Clark tracked down a century-old multi-denominational parish story and helped to prompt our shared research path.

ACKNOWLEDGMENTS

Particular thanks are due to the Sorting Hat at Warner Bros. Studios in Burbank, which pronounced us each Gryffindor and spurred us to dare to work together.

Special appreciation goes to Margaret Shannon and John Budde, whose editing skills helped ensure a readable copy. Any errors that remain are entirely our own.

Our families cheered us all along the way. Our spouses, Bill Richards, John Budde, and Carolyn McDonald, each walked this journey with us, encouraging, forbearing, and making it possible for us to pursue this project. To them, our partners in life and faith, we offer thanks too deep for words.

Introduction

If we accept division from other Christians as normal and inevitable, we turn away from the mission God has given us.

In One Body through the Cross, para. 19

A TREASURE HIDDEN IN A FIELD

Christian worshiping communities number in the hundreds of thousands across the United States and Canada. Sprinkled among them are congregations with a distinct character. They have dared to share. That is, they have constituted themselves multi-denominationally. Refusing to accept division from other Christians as "normal and inevitable," they live out their faith lives in covenanted partnership, sharing worship and ministry while remaining in good standing with the two or more denominations they formally represent. Currently, there are over 500 such congregations in the United States and about 100 in Canada. This book explores the phenomenon of multi-denominational congregations. It describes who they are, why and how they form and develop, and their special contributions to the search for Christian unity.

Like a treasure hidden in a field, these congregations, and those who serve them, sparkle with promise. They model daily respect and dialogue across difference in a divided society. They share resources in ways that strengthen and enable mission and witness. By their inclusive nature they become beacons of welcome and hope for individuals and communities. Of course, they also struggle with all the usual issues of congregational life and with the special complications of their multi-denominational reality. However, their members often experience even the challenges as gifts. A lay member of

1

one multi-denominational parish states, "The one thing we have in common is a faith in Jesus Christ. And how that is expressed is free and open, which allows, in my opinion, for a much deeper personal study and a respect communally for the differences."[1]

To study multi-denominational congregations fully is to undertake a multi-faceted task. It needs to capture their experience in vivid and honest ways. It needs to explain how they operate and relate to the wider church. It needs to assess their theological implications for divided Christianity. This book is thus in part a collection of stories—the rich narratives, past and present, of these unique entities. It is also an educational resource, offering tools for creating and maintaining them. It is also a work of ecclesiology, seeking to learn from these lived expressions of Christian cooperation something new about the nature of the church itself. While each chapter tends to prioritize one of these facets, they also weave around each other throughout the book. Further, the authors represent two countries, and three different Christian denominations: Mitzi the Evangelical Lutheran Church in America, Sandra the United Church of Canada, and William the United Methodist Church. Each author has taken the lead in drafting chapters, but the voices of all three are threaded throughout. The book, like the parishes it studies, is the fruitful outcome of the ecumenical exchange of gifts for the building of Christ's body.

In the rest of this Introduction, we set the stage for the study of multi-denominational congregations, first by defining them, then by telling briefly the history of multi-denominational formation in the United States and Canada and inviting readers to consider the possibilities they hold for the twenty-first century. After a note on the authors' research methods, the book takes on its three tasks: introducing the various models of multi-denominational congregations in Part I, describing aspects of their lives and governance in Part II, and, finally, delving into the questions of theology and ecclesiology that they pose—and sometimes answer—in Part III.

DEFINING MULTI-DENOMINATIONAL CONGREGATIONS

At its most basic, a multi-denominational congregation is one in which at least two denominations worship and serve God in a unified way, while still maintaining their respective denominational identities and connections. Any combination of denominations might share a program, mission, ministry, or building. This book focuses on congregational ministries, particularly those where sharing has deepened into full integration, one where the congregation

---

1. Sunriver Christian Fellowship, Boubel, interview.

shares ministry personnel and worships together, having committed to one another through the signing of a covenant or constitution. Unlike autonomous community churches, these parishes, through their covenanted relationships, choose to remain in good standing with their judicatories.

Diverse nomenclature for such congregations—multi-denominational parishes, inter-church congregations, ecumenical shared ministries, union churches, federated congregations, or cooperative parishes—can make the topic confusing. In Canada, they are generally called "ecumenical shared ministry" (ESM) congregations. No matter how they choose to describe themselves, their commonality is in covenanting together for worship, service, mission, and faith nurture across two or more denominational traditions. They come in many flavors. In the United States, these congregations represent mainly combinations of these churches:

- The Episcopal Church (TEC)
- Evangelical Lutheran Church of America (ELCA)
- Presbyterian Church USA (PCUSA)
- United Church of Christ

In Canada, the primary partners include:

- Anglican Church of Canada (ACC)
- Evangelical Lutheran Church in Canada (ELCIC)
- Presbyterian Church in Canada PCIC)
- The United Church of Canada (UCC)

Several North American partnerships include:

- The Christian Church (Disciples of Christ)
- Roman Catholic Church
- Mennonite Church Canada
- Unitarian Church
- Baptists
- Moravian Church in North America

A BRIEF HISTORY OF MULTI-DENOMINATIONAL SHARING

What is the origin of these sharing relationships? While each parish has its own birth story, discernible trends have led to the emergence of these parishes at different times in Christian history. Early forms of parish cooperation included the *Simultankirchen*, sixteenth- century congregations scattered across Germany, where Roman Catholic, Lutheran, and Reformed traditions shared the church building in the wake of the Protestant Reformation. Some continue to this day, e.g., Michaeliskirche (St. Michael's) in Hildesheim, founded in 1542.

Further economic and social upheavals led to immigration within Europe and beyond. In the early nineteenth century in South Russia, congregations of migrant German farmers combined their Lutheran and Reformed traditions and called one pastor between them. Similar sharing arrangements had begun even earlier among German immigrants to the rolling hills of Pennsylvania and with Swedish Lutherans and Anglicans along the Delaware River.

By the late nineteenth century, the nascent ecumenical movement helped lead Protestant churches to recognize that competing missions were not only expensive but also damaging to the cause of the gospel. The challenges of providing resources, including clergy, for the westward expansion of the churches across the North American continent led to the possibility of working together. Episcopalians and Lutherans in the United States and Methodists and Presbyterians in Canada hammered out comity agreements, pledging to plant churches in places that would not compete with the other denomination. In 1886, a Presbyterian sent from eastern Canada to minister at Lethbridge, in western Canada, reported: "The greatest harmony prevails between the different denominations. The resident clergy . . . are as Jonathan and David. . . . All sheep-stealing is to be abolished and we think we will have enough to do in fighting his Satanic Majesty without fighting each other."[2]

POST–WORLD WAR II DEVELOPMENTS

With some exceptions, the ecumenical spirit that blossomed immediately after the Second World War failed to fuel broader multi-denominational congregational formation. However, ecumenical work continued. Multi-denominational congregations today stem mostly from the 1960s onward, when combined influences of economic and social changes and increasing

---

2. Fennell, "Rev. McKillop's Diary," 40.

ecumenical commitments—especially with the full entry of Roman Catholics into ecumenical life as a result of the Second Vatican Council. Dozens of bilateral dialogues began among Roman Catholic, Protestant, and Orthodox denominations, often leading to ecumenical congregational sharing between Roman Catholic and Protestant and Anglican partners. In Canada, a combination of ecumenical enthusiasm and the desire and need to work together to serve newly emerging resource towns (especially in mining and hydroelectric power generation) led to the first wave of contemporary multi-denominational congregations in the 1960s and 1970s.

The late 1990s and early 2000s featured the emergence of several interdenominational "full communion" agreements. In the United States, these agreements were ratified among the Reformed family of churches with the Evangelical Lutheran Church in America (1997) and between ELCA Lutherans and The Episcopal Church (2001), followed by United Methodists and the Evangelical Lutheran Church in America (2009). In Canada, the Anglican Church of Canada and the Evangelical Lutheran Church in Canada came into full communion in 2001. These denominational partnerships have fostered support for, and mutual responsibility toward one another, at the judicatory level, leading to a new wave of multi-denominational congregations in Canada and the United States.

While impulses toward building a shared ministry have arisen from pastoral or judicatory (oversight) leadership in some places, or the simple desire of people to worship, learn, and serve together as members of two or more traditions, most have been formed out of economic necessity. For instance, small Presbyterian and United Church of Christ congregations might struggle alone a few blocks from one another in an urban area. One can no longer support a pastor; the other cannot maintain its facility. Members of each, who have known one another for decades, begin talking together about what it would take for them to come together as a shared ministry, able to be and do more together than they would apart. Hearts and minds generate enthusiasm and a plan for coming together while sharing and preserving the treasures of each congregation's history, character, worship style, and theological stance. A multi-denominational ministry is born.

A MODEL FOR THE TWENTY-FIRST CENTURY CHURCH?

The discoveries made on this journey into multi-denominational parish life will provide seminarians, clergy and lay leaders, and denominational judicatory heads with examples showing how the formal theological agreements of Christian churches are being lived out in local mission and ministry in new and creative ways across the church. We also hope to reach church leaders at local, regional, and national levels with information that will inform, assist, and spur their thinking about and consideration of ecumenical ministry possibilities.

Where such parishes already exist, this book will equip congregations and judicatory leaders for their further formation and flourishing. These congregations can impact future ministries, providing a fresh expression of the local church's mission and ministry for the twenty-first century. Assessing the mission of these churches opens a window on their practices and the challenges they face. It can inspire and challenge "the usual way of being the church" as so often lived out in dutifully isolated local assemblies.

We three authors share a realistic and hopeful perspective on the place of multi-denominational congregations on the complex map of twenty-first century Christianity in the United States and Canada. These churches, which have all experienced times of trial and triumph, invite creative theological reflection on the very foundations of Christianity "where two or three are gathered." Above all, these churches have merited our investigation because they have dared to imagine church in brave and new ways. We believe that as more Christians discover how these congregations of Jesus' followers are bravely living out his call to be one, they will take up the dare.

Listen with us to their voices.

A Note on Research Methodology

MULTIDISCIPLINARY INQUIRY

LIKE THE MULTI-DENOMINATIONAL CONGREGATIONS this book describes, our research and topics cross disciplinary boundaries. As we have noted, the research is theological and ethnographic; the topics are practical, pastoral, and ecclesiological. In our research, we draw upon literature in the fields of congregational studies, ecumenical theology and ecclesiology, and ecumenical reception. We look to theories of cultural hybridity, place, and multiple religious belonging. Our ethnographic work was conversational, observational, and attentive to community and context. It focused on practices (worship, education, nurture, organization) and theological questions (how these parishes reconcile denominational differences in socioeconomic contexts, missional needs, and ethical concerns).

VISITS, INTERVIEWS, AND ONLINE SURVEY

Our research included site visits, observation, and in-depth interviews with clergy and laity in congregations in different regions, contexts, and denominational combinations.[1] As this project involved research with human subjects, it used an ethical protocol for interviews that was approved by the ethics review committee of the Saskatoon Theological Union, following the national standards set out for the humanities in the Canadian Tri-Council Guidelines for Research Using Human Subjects. The first wave of research involved contacts with 127 clergy in the United States and 67 in Canada to study these parishes' histories and socioeconomic contexts, missional needs, and other

1. The key guides for the ethnographic protocol were Madden, *Being Ethnographic*; and Moschella, *Ethnography as a Pastoral Practice*.

contingencies that led to the formation of these congregations across North America.

Two online surveys, one of thirty-one congregations in the US and one of sixty-seven in Canada, collected information on features of congregational life such as worship, education, and nurture. Additionally, one of the co-authors moderated an electronic forum where respondents could reflect on their congregational narratives, learn from others, and grow in awareness about their respective missions.

Parish Visits

Taken together, the three authors visited and conducted interviews at thirty-two multi-denominational parishes. The congregations selected for on-site visits reflected different geographic and cultural contexts and various denominational combinations. We developed a visit protocol, including standard interview procedures and questions for clergy, lay members, and judicatories. At each visit, we conducted interviews with the parish clergy and groups of lay leaders, and we observed the parish at worship. Like all research, ethnography is not completely neutral observation; it is not possible to be the proverbial "fly on the wall" and overhear conversations as they would occur naturally in these ministry contexts.

During parish visits and interviews, certain realities became manifest. The authors sought to be attentive to the impact of this research project upon the churches themselves. Just the fact that a researcher had traveled to a parish to study its history, current situation, and community life in an in-depth way had an impact in and of itself (the Hawthorne effect). Several parishes expressed surprise and delight that they were known beyond the local community and deemed "worthy" to be included in the study. One layperson said, "I am glad that we hung in there because your project shows that it was worth it. Someone has taken notice. . . . After this long, something being here is recognized as, oh, somebody thought it was a good idea twenty-some years ago, and they still do, so maybe it is. I am hoping that what this community can do in the future is to let people know that it is possible."[2]

Interviews

Further, we recognize that all research flows from the people interviewed. What we found results from those with whom we spoke. Often the clergy

2. Spirit of Grace at Mission of the Atonement, Cannard, interview.

person had carefully selected the laity to be interviewed about the ecumenical shared ministry at their parish, seeking a demographic balance of long-term members and newcomers. Those chosen were often particularly reflective and theologically articulate. We are aware that, at times, this may have resulted in a halo effect.

The ministers' attitude toward the study elicited a range of responses. Some were welcoming from the initial contact. Others, cautiously receptive at first contact, became increasingly interested and engaged as the study progressed. A few clergy became hesitant or resistant to our questions, and in one instance, a clergy person agreed to participate in the interview process, but then was nowhere to be found when the researcher arrived at the parish after traveling five hours for the appointment. However, most of the participating clergy were frank and forthcoming. The laity clearly enjoyed hearing one another reflect on their shared lived experience in the group interviews. In fact, at the end of an hour-long interview, when the researcher said, "Before I turn off the recorder, is there anything you wanted to say that I did not ask or you did not have the opportunity to say?" the conversation would often continue for another ten or fifteen minutes.

In our visits, the theme of authenticity and commitment surfaced frequently. One layperson said:

> We have always been kind of a multi-denominational family. Over time what has really kept us here is the community, the people, the authenticity, the honesty, the intellectual challenge, the acceptance, and things that other people have been saying that just keep stimulating us to want to stay. . . . It is not the denomination . . . being Catholic, Lutheran, or whatever, it is the mix in the kind of stew of all these different faith traditions that I think makes it really rich for us here.[3]

This book invites readers to observe these places of authenticity and commitment for themselves.

---

3. Spirit of Grace at Mission of the Atonement, Buesseler, interview.

PART I

Models

1

Full Communion Parishes

"GET READY FOR SOMETHING BIG": THE CHURCH OF THE NATIVITY, BALTIMORE

Baptism Sundays, even snowy ones, tend to draw visitors, and Sunday, March 1, 2015 at the Episcopal Church of the Holy Comforter in Cedarcroft, a northern suburb of Baltimore, was no exception. But this visitor was different: he was a scout from a neighboring parish, Nativity Lutheran Church. Now only a small remnant of fifty from its heyday of 550 members, the tiny, faithful Nativity community had decided to leave its large, 1950s building and seek a community to join. Staying together as a worshiping community was their new mission, giving up the fight with deferred maintenance, a failing boiler, and high utility bills. The beloved building had become their albatross. "The building was going to pull us down and drown us. We decided that the most important thing was staying together as a congregation. There was a lot of love for the building, but we gave it up."[1] In preparation, the pastor, the Rev. David Eisenhuth, sent out visitors to scout neighboring parishes, both sister Lutherans and cousins of other denominational bodies.

Simultaneously yet independently, the Rev. Stewart Lucas, the young energetic rector of the Episcopal Church of the Holy Comforter, had been

---

1. Church of the Nativity and Holy Comforter, Valentine, interview with the Lutheran Episcopal Coordinating Committee of the Metropolitan Washington, DC Synod, Diocese of Washington and Diocese of Virginia. The Lutheran church building was subsequently sold to Faith Triumphant Ministries International.

watching and waiting. He had come to Holy Comforter two years before with the audacious goal of doubling the size of this dwindling parish. In two years, the congregation had grown from fifty to sixty-six. Unsure how to proceed, Father Lucas nevertheless felt led to "get ready for something big," so the congregation spent time and energy on their early twentieth-century building, cleaning out closets, repairing sidewalks, and painting classrooms in this attractive Tudor stucco church and school complex. Now they prayerfully waited.

At Holy Comforter on that snowy Sunday in March, the scout, Jeff Valentine, found a community that felt like family: welcoming, ethnically diverse, of similar size and social location to Nativity. When Jeff discovered that the woman in the pew behind him at worship was a member of the vestry, he told her why he was there. "That's funny," she said, "just yesterday the vestry had a retreat to determine what we want to be when we grow up!" Eight months later to the day, on All Saints Sunday, November 1, 2015, the two parishes celebrated their first service as a new Lutheran-Episcopal joint parish, the Church of the Nativity and Holy Comforter. A representative from each of the two parishes poured water into the baptismal font, symbolizing their coming together in ecclesial partnership.

"The reason it has worked thus far," said Father Lucas, "is that both have followed the leading of the Spirit. We have honored that inkling and guidance every step of the way, and we have gotten out of the way sometimes. We've made room for stuff we wouldn't have otherwise. . . . It's all about relationships."[2] However, similar congregational demographics were also important. Both congregations were diverse in racial, ethnic, economic status, and sexual identities. According to the church's publicity about the partnership: "Both are committed to welcoming the stranger, the traveler, and the immigrant."[3] Finding shared culture has been the key to discerning a shared ministry.

This chapter explores various models of interchurch congregations whose denominations are in full communion partnerships. This is the newest model of multi-denominational ministry, and these are the easiest joint parishes to form because they are living out the strategic commitments of the national churches on the ground. Still, they have their own distinct challenges and opportunities. Below, we explore the distinctive features of four congregations that are full communion shared ministries. We look at the trends and

---

2. Church of the Nativity and Holy Comforter, Lucas, interview with the Lutheran Episcopal Coordinating Committee of the Metropolitan Washington, DC Synod, Diocese of Washington and Diocese of Virginia.

3. "FAQs about the Nativity-Holy Comforter Joint Ministry."

patterns that reveal the graces—and the trials—of this model of parish life, and we explore the promise of this model for the future of the church.

DEFINING FULL COMMUNION

The Evangelical Lutheran Church in America (ELCA) defines full communion as the goal of the ecumenical movement. Its policy statement adopted in 1991, *Ecumenism: The Vision of the Evangelical Lutheran Church in America*, defines "full communion" in powerful terms:

> Full communion, a gift from God, is founded on faith in Jesus Christ. It is a commitment to truth in love and a witness to God's liberation and reconciliation. Full communion is visible and sacramental. . . . [It] points to the complete communion and unity of all Christians that will come with the arrival of the kingdom of God at the parousia of Christ, the Lord. It is also a goal in need of continuing definition. It is rooted in agreement on essentials and allows diversity in nonessentials.[4]

The ELCA has established full communion agreements with the Reformed family (the Presbyterian Church USA, the Reformed Church in America, and the United Church of Christ [1997]); the Moravian Church of America, Northern and Southern Provinces (1999); The Episcopal Church (2001); and the United Methodist Church (2009). The Episcopal Church is party to five full communion agreements. The Episcopal-Evangelical Lutheran Church in America full communion agreement, *Called to Common Mission*, describes the unity and diversity at the heart of full communion: "Within this new relation, churches become interdependent while remaining autonomous. . . . Diversity is preserved, but this diversity is not static. Neither church seeks to remake the other in its own image, but each is open to the gifts of the other as it seeks to be faithful to Christ and his mission."[5]

To date, there is only one full communion partnership within the Canadian church family: the Waterloo Declaration, signed in 2001 between the Anglican Church of Canada and the Evangelical Lutheran Church in Canada. Like its US counterparts, the Waterloo Declaration commits the two denominations to ongoing mutuality in ministry, worship, and witness.

---

4. Evangelical Lutheran Church in America, *Ecumenism*, 13.

5. Episcopal Church and Evangelical Lutheran Church in America, "Called to Common Mission."

The ELCA's full communion agreements with the Episcopal Church, the Moravian Church, and the United Methodist Church each respectively identify six characteristics of full communion:

- Common confession of faith;

- Mutual recognition of baptism and Eucharist, enabling joint worship and membership exchange;

- Mutual recognition of clergy, subject to the regulations of mutual polity;

- Shared evangelism, witness, and service;

- Common decision-making on critical common issues of faith and life;

- Mutual lifting of any condemnations that exist between the churches.

The *Formula of Agreement* between the ELCA and the Reformed family of churches adds a seventh characteristic of full communion, in which the parties "pledge themselves to living together under the Gospel in such a way that the principle of mutual affirmation and admonition becomes the basis of a trusting relationship in which respect and love for the other will have a chance to grow."[6]

This model assumes that common mission means full partnership at the parish level. The US Lutheran-Episcopal asset map lists eighty-four joint Episcopal Church-Evangelical Lutheran Church in America ministries.[7] Among these are trailblazers: Lamb of God in Fort Myers, Florida; Sunriver Christian Fellowship in Sunriver, Oregon; the Church of the Good Shepherd in Galax, Virginia; and in Canada, Grace St. John's Anglican Lutheran Church in Carman, Manitoba; and St. Andrew's Trinity Anglican Lutheran Church in Rosetown, Saskatchewan. Their local partnerships preceded—and seeded—the denominations' ratification of the full communion agreement. They demonstrated that differences could and should be bridged before the national full communion agreements came into being. Many more have been formed since. In Canada, there are about twenty-five covenanted Anglican/Lutheran shared ministries. Anglicans and Lutherans also participate in a number of three-party ecumenical parishes across Canada.

Full communion ecumenical parishes already have full approval for clergy to serve in each other's churches and to celebrate the sacraments using the other church's liturgies. They also have full exchangeability of lay members, with full recognition of baptisms and confirmations. They have the freedom to

6. Evangelical Lutheran Church in America, the Presbyterian Church (USA), Reformed Church in America, and United Church of Christ, *Formula of Agreement*.

7. Episcopal Shared Ministry Asset Map.

use both churches' liturgies and, often further, the latitude to create a blended liturgy from the resources of both churches. And they enjoy built-in full reciprocity of the sacrament of the Eucharist.

Because of the full communion relationship between ELCA Lutherans and Episcopalians, additional structures are in place: a community of similar parishes, a national coordinating committee to encourage and publicize the work, and support structures, such as a Facebook page for clergy serving these ministries. Coordinated funding makes outreach ministries possible. In Winston-Salem, North Carolina, for example, the local Lutheran synod and Episcopal diocese in 2016 collaboratively established and funded a Latino-African-American joint mission, the Comunidad Amada de Cristo/Christ's Beloved Community. The Slate Project, based in Baltimore, is an experimental Lutheran-Episcopal alternative Christian community that combines face-to-face gatherings with a digital community participating synchronously and asynchronously from around the globe.

Full communion ecumenical parishes also have the advantage of relatively compatible polities. The role of respective bishops (or corresponding role of *episcopé* such as presbytery) has been worked out at the national level. Each full communion agreement has a document guiding the *Orderly Exchange* of clergy under the agreement.[8] In Canada, a Joint Anglican Lutheran Commission supports local ministries, and in 2006, produced a resource to assist the formation of shared ministry partnerships.[9]

FULL COMMUNION, PLUS OTHERS TOO: SUNRIVER CHRISTIAN FELLOWSHIP, SUNRIVER, OREGON

Since ecumenical shared ministry congregations are by nature diverse and welcoming, they tend to attract members beyond their covenanted partnerships. Full communion ministries thus find themselves ministering with Christians of other backgrounds. Sometimes these ministries expand officially to form multi-denominational ministries (see chapter 4). In many other situations, the two-way partnership finds creative ways to welcome and include these other Christians. Seasonal resort communities have proven to be fertile ground for such ecumenical shared ministries, often providing the only mainline denominational presence in town. The skiing resort communities of Big Sky, Montana and Sunriver, Oregon are home to thriving Lutheran-Episcopal

8. For example, Episcopal Church and the Evangelical Lutheran Church, *Orderly Exchange of Pastors.*

9. Joint Anglican Lutheran Commission, "Guidelines."

ecumenical shared parishes that serve not only ELCA Lutherans and Episcopalians, but also many other mainline denominational folk as well, such as Presbyterians, Methodists, Disciples, and Baptists. These parishes face the contingencies of any resort town ministry: drastic seasonal changes in attendance, part-time members who spend half of the year elsewhere, and an older, wealthier demographic. But they have distinctive challenges and opportunities as well.

The national churches' work toward a full communion relationship was the impetus for the formation of the joint Lutheran-Episcopal Sunriver Christian Fellowship in the resort community of Sunriver, Oregon. An Episcopal priest, the Rev. Nancy McGrath-Green, was serving the two communities separately as a shared clergyperson. It was her vision to bring the two congregations together for joint worship. Founded in 1996, Sunriver Christian Fellowship was an experiment in anticipation of the full communion accord adopted in 2001 between the ELCA and the Episcopal Church. At first, the joint group met in the community nature center. Then the local Roman Catholic bishop, who wanted to establish a parish in Sunriver, invited them into a partnership. They bought a building together and shared the renovation. Looking back, the parish believes the key to this model was that all three of the then-bishops—Lutheran, Episcopal, and Roman Catholic—were willing to work in new ways in order to come up with this creative agreement. Now Sunriver Christian Fellowship is a joint Lutheran-Episcopal parish that rents space in Holy Trinity Roman Catholic Church.

Although officially a Lutheran-Episcopal parish, the Sunriver Christian Fellowship membership today is forty percent Lutheran-Episcopal and sixty percent "other." Presbyterians make up nearly half of the "other" category; the rest are Baptist, Disciples, Methodist, and former Catholics. One member even wrote a song about being a "Catho-luth-episcopalian-presbyterian." The Rev. McGrath-Green leads alternating Lutheran and Episcopal liturgies twice per month. One Sunday per month they use Iona or Taize or another varied liturgy. The fourth Sunday worship is led by a cadre of retired clergy who are parish members, who preside at worship using their own liturgical tradition— American Baptist, Disciples of Christ, Presbyterian, Lutheran, or Episcopal.

"At Sunriver Christian Fellowship, there is no delineation between the Catholics, the Presbyterians, the Lutherans, the Episcopalians," a lay member said. "More or less, the one thing we have in common is a faith in Jesus Christ. And how that is expressed is free and open, which allows for (in my opinion) a much deeper, personal study and a respect communally for the differences."[10] Another member adds, "In my perspective we focus on our commonality,

10. Sunriver Christian Fellowship, Boubel, interview.

which is ninety-eight, ninety-nine percent." As for the two-percent difference, "there is a very high degree of receptive tolerance."[11] As they attract
other Christians, ecumenical shared ministry parishes need to address both
the desire to be inclusive and embracing and the commitment to their formal
denominational covenants. We discuss this issue further as we look at governance in chapter 8.

The biggest challenges that full communion multi-denominational parishes face are the same as all shared ministry congregations: merging their
identities, defining who they are as a new congregational entity, developing
a shared vision for mission, designing new worship practices, and addressing
governance in two denominational modes. Although the two denominations
have agreed that they share a great deal of the gospel and its mission, putting
those noble phrases into action can still be complex and sometimes bewilder-
ing. If the impetus to share ministry has begun from the church's judicatories,
it may be difficult to transfer that enthusiasm to the members of the congregation. We now look at some of the ways full communion shared ministries face
these issues.

MERGING IDENTITIES: SPIRIT OF GRACE, WEST BLOOMFIELD, MICHIGAN

The culture of ecumenical shared parishes requires a certain kind of openness
to a new and complex identity: "How do you cope with the change in your
congregational identity? What is your new identity?"[12] Spirit of Grace is an
Evangelical Lutheran Church in America-Episcopal Church ecumenical parish in West Bloomfield, Michigan, a suburb of Detroit. Once three congregations, they were brought together by the Spirit with financial exigency as the
catalyst. In September 2012, Advent Episcopal Church lost its $1.2 million
new building due to a financing disaster. The nearby Sylvan Lake Lutheran
congregation invited Advent to join them, first sharing their worship space at
separate times, then soon thereafter beginning to worship together. Another
small neighboring congregation, Ascension Lutheran, joined the partnership.
They slowly integrated their ministries ("integrating the altar guides was revo-
lutionary," their former priest/pastor said[13]), and gradually worked to merge

---

11. Sunriver Christian Fellowship, Adams, interview.

12. Church of the Epiphany, Perez, interview.

13. Spirit of Grace, West Bloomfield, Dostert, presentation to Lutheran Episcopal Coordinating Committee.

into a joint Lutheran-Episcopal parish. By April 2015, they had adopted Articles of Federation.

This dynamic, energetic group prayed and discerned with great intentionality over merging three congregations together into one unified body. Most of the parishioners are deeply committed to this new paradigm, even as they have faced the growing pains. The Episcopalians, for example, experienced significant grief over losing their beautiful sanctuary. Giving up their "idolatry of the architecture," they had to come to terms with moving into and sharing a more modest 1950s-era church building. A reality that these blended parishes face early on is duplication of staffing as the churches merge together. At Spirit of Grace, the clergy had to put their calls on the table; one left for another call soon thereafter.

Some parishes uphold the individual denominational identities and view the ecumenical partnership as strengthening those identities. Others intentionally downplay the partner denominations in favor of a new blended identity. And some parishes have a mixture of opinions within the parish itself around the question of denominational identity. While some parishioners assert a strong attachment to their denominational affiliations, other feel they have blended identities. As one parishioner put it:

> I think that I am now officially a Luthepalian. But I think the analogy is really one of a marriage. You are bringing two different backgrounds together, and you do not lose that, but you do become a Luthepalian. You have a unity of your own. . . . The important thing I think for anybody—whether they be a pastor or whatever—is to recognize Christ within each other. I think that is key.[14]

As in a marriage, the discussion and discernment process around naming the newly formed or newly merged ecumenical church entity is symbolic of the search for identity. The Lutherans and Episcopalians who came together in West Bloomfield described an extensive participatory process over choosing their new church name, Spirit of Grace. At first, everyone who attended church or who used the church building (e.g. the AA group, the exercise group) was invited to suggest a name for the new entity. When the list grew to an overwhelming 106 names, the process was scrapped and restarted. The choir and the youth group weighed in. "We have given time for everyone in the congregation to take a pause and to listen," said lay leader Susan Fine, describing the long, convoluted process of discernment. "We have been transparent in our communication and allowed everybody to listen to each other's

---

14. Spirit of Grace, West Bloomfield, Van Blarcum, interview.

thoughts and to ponder what is the best for us and let the Holy Spirit direct us in all of our decisions. I think the most important thing we have done in this whole process is embrace diversity, listen to each other, and let the Holy Spirit lead us."[15] This kind of extensive collaborative listening and discernment process came up time and time again as vital in order for these shared ministry situations to survive and thrive.

IMAGING WHO WE ARE—THE POWER OF SYMBOL

The Cedarcroft, Maryland parish went a step further, commissioning a professional graphic designer to create an image for the new Lutheran-Episcopal ministry, a graphic that combines the Episcopal shield and the Luther rose. For the inaugural worship service of the new ecumenical partnership, each parishioner received a new name tag, incorporating the new logo. The rack of name tags was the first thing parishioners saw when they walked through the doors for the first joint worship service. Father Lucas said, "The logo was the best money we spent. The name tag change and having them in the rack on the first day was a more powerful symbol than I could have imagined."[16] These name tags symbolized that parishioners' primary identity was/is in their baptismal identity as Christians and that their denominational identities were and are important, but secondary. The primacy of baptismal identity was further symbolized as the first worship service of the newly created Lutheran-Episcopal congregation opened with an Affirmation of Baptism. During that liturgy, water from the Lutherans' former baptismal font was poured into the font of their new church home, so that old and new baptismal waters commingled, a powerful symbol of new unity.

DEVELOPING A SHARED VISION FOR MISSION: SPIRIT OF GRACE, HOOD RIVER, OREGON

The Lutheran-Episcopal full communion agreement is aptly titled *Called to Common Mission* since discerning mission together is a key challenge for these ecumenical shared ministry parishes. The Rev. Stephen Bancroft from Spirit of Grace Church in West Bloomfield said, "We are being challenged, I think, to look at every aspect of who we are and how we do it with an entire new vision. . . . Our mission, in my opinion, is incredibly powerful, and it was

15. Spirit of Grace, West Bloomfield, Fine, interview.

16. Church of the Nativity and Holy Comforter, Lucas, interview with the National Lutheran Episcopal Coordinating Committee.

put together by the laity of this church. I just think it is a powerful process. We will never be the same again. Never."[17]

The United Methodist-Evangelical Lutheran Church in America joint parish in Hood River, Oregon successfully brought an ecumenical parish into being, despite significant conflict over becoming a two-denomination parish. The two merging congregations of the Hood River Lutheran-Methodist joint parish had long and rich histories. Asbury United Methodist Church in Hood River, Oregon was a 125-year-old congregation that had courageously stood in solidarity with those of Japanese descent during World War II, a highly unpopular stance in Oregon at that time. With its building deteriorating and its congregation dwindling, Asbury was on the verge of closure. Our Redeemer Lutheran Church was a fifty-year old congregation with a passion for the community food bank ministry, but with shrinking resources and few members. The two parishes began exploring the possibility of a partnership in January 2010. The UMC congregation sold their building, and the Lutheran building is now the home of the joint UMC-ELCA parish. The initial partnership was a two-year trial agreement that began in 2013. "What we are hoping to be is according to the ELCA a federated congregation,[18] and according to the United Methodist Church a union congregation, which means that we are one congregation," explained the pastor, the Rev. David King. "Everyone who is a member of this congregation is a member of an ELCA church *and* a member of the United Methodist Church."[19] Two years later, after a four-month congregational listening process, they adopted the constitution and became one congregation related to two denominational bodies.

In the midst of this extended and sometimes conflicted merging process, which included a change of clergy leadership, this congregation simultaneously devoted itself to fundraising and building a new $1 million food bank. They provided the land and led the process to create a state-of-the-art community building, with a large warehouse, multiple industrial refrigerators, a client area for food distribution, a children's zone, and a commercial kitchen for food preparation classes. The church's backyard was converted into a large garden to supply the food bank.

The vision and mission of the food-bank project was the impetus to work through their differences during the merger process. "It was really nice to have something else to focus on," one parishioner said. "I do not know that I could have stuck through and made it through the nastiness if there had not been something else to focus on and to work toward. There already was a

17. Spirit of Grace, West Bloomfield, Bancroft, interview.

18. Evangelical Lutheran Church in America, "Documents of Governance and Policy."

19. Spirit of Grace, Hood River, King, interview.

goal, and I could see a mission happening somewhere. It seemed like a relief to have somewhere else to focus for me personally."[20] Visionary leadership from beyond the congregations was also central to the ultimate success of this endeavor. "The two things that kept us getting back on track were the vision of the Fish building, the food bank, and the mentoring, coaching, running interference of the synod bishop and the district superintendent," another parishioner explained. "They were tremendously helpful and spent quite a bit of time here. I think it helped that some of the folks who had the greatest fears about the merger worked very, very hard on the food-bank building committee. And I think that helped, too, because they had a mission to accomplish. It was just exciting."[21]

Another example of mission driving and sustaining partnership may be found at Grace Mountainside Church (ELCA-Episcopal), located in Appalachia in the poorest county in North Carolina. A hallmark of this parish's identity is the community soup kitchen. The only church in the area offering this kind of ministry, Grace has discerned a mission to feed people physically as well as spiritually, and seeks to offer a different form of Christianity to the community. In a similar vein, Sunriver Christian Fellowship in Oregon has found that not owning real estate frees them to use their finances for outreach. The parish has an extensive array of local and global outreach programs. "This parish cherishes its environment and understands creation and stewardship," said a lay member. "It has an incredibly committed outreach on so many programs at the local level, from providing appropriate underwear for children in grade schools who do not have it, to providing water in third-world countries so that they can have clean water."[22] Such a vision for mission and outreach is vital to the flourishing of these shared ministries.

WORSHIP: BLENDED OR ALTERNATING?

While full communion agreements facilitate shared worship, uniting two long-established but dwindling parishes can bring up parishioners' grief and lost hope for recovery of how the church once was. And often, this grief focuses around worship practices. The United Methodist-Evangelical Lutheran Church in America congregation in Hood River has chosen not to have distinctly Lutheran services and Methodist services, but rather traditional and contemporary services that alternate using liturgies and music from both

20. Spirit of Grace, Hood River, Boris, interview.
21. Spirit of Grace, Hood River, Chenoweth, interview.
22. Sunriver Christian Fellowship, Adams, interview.

denominations. Sometimes parishioners express nostalgia for their former worship traditions: "I would say people voiced it as being afraid of losing their Lutheran-ness or their Methodist identities. And where that most came out was in worship styles. . . . I think that was an easy place for people to put their fears. . . . It certainly helped when we moved to two services. We tried really hard not to have a Lutheran service and a Methodist service, but a traditional and more contemporary service. But I don't know that we have totally re-solved that issue of identity and wanting to identify as a United Methodist or wanting to identify as a Lutheran."[23] However, as people experienced wor-ship together, over time they came to identify the gifts and graces in the new ecumenical parish worship experience. "I think there was real joy in terms of combined worship and increased numbers and more voices singing together and more people praying together," one lay leader observed. "I think that was tremendous."[24]

Some US Lutheran-Episcopal and Canadian Anglican-Lutheran parishes have designed blended liturgies that use elements of both Lutheran and Epis-copal or Anglican liturgies in every service. For Episcopalians and Anglicans, this requires the permission of the local diocesan bishop. Other full commu-nion ecumenical parishes have chosen to keep the denominational liturgies intact and to rotate usage. Sunriver Christian Fellowship, for example, does so by alternating weeks. Other parishes rotate their use of respective denomi-national liturgies by liturgical season. We explore the important questions of ecumenical liturgical life further in chapter 7.

Confirmation is a challenge for shared parishes whose traditions have significant differences such as how long confirmation preparation should take and what material should be covered in confirmation classes. The question of who confirms whom is a particularly vexed question, because in most Prot-estant traditions, the local pastor confirms, while Episcopal/Anglican canons require that the diocesan bishop confirm. There are various ways in which full communion parishes attempt to bridge this difference in normative prac-tice. Some joint parishes have the local pastor/priest and the Episcopal bishop jointly confirm all the confirmands; some coordinate a visit of both Episcopal bishops and the other denomination's bishops or judicatory leaders for confir-mation; and others have the Episcopal bishop confirm the Episcopalians and the local pastor confirm the others. We consider some of the implications of membership and confirmation in chapter 11.

---

23. Spirit of Grace, Hood River, Boris, interview.

24. Spirit of Grace, Hood River, Chenoweth, interview.

FEDERATION VIS-À-VIS CANONS

For many ecumenical shared parishes, the legalities over a parish constitution and bylaws, a unified budget, and property matters can be the biggest challenge in forming a partnership. Even with a full communion covenant, getting an approved constitution or articles of incorporation document can be difficult in agreements involving the Episcopal or Anglican Church, as diocesan chancellors often find the proposals incompatible with the assumptions built into Episcopal/Anglican canon law. Work-arounds such as letters of agreement for parishes DBA (doing business as) another entity can require expensive legal work. Jim Van Blarcum at Spirit of Grace in West Bloomfield articulated well what many parishioners expressed, "The process more or less was the big thing to overcome, not ourselves or our faith."[25] The governance chapter later in this book offers strategies and structures that have worked as solutions for some shared parishes.

STEPPING OUT IN FAITH

Ecumenical shared parishes are first and foremost Christian communities with the same mission and focus as all other Christian congregations: to preach the gospel and celebrate the sacraments, to minister to one another in time of need, to reach out in mission and ministry to the local and global community in Christ's name. What is distinctive about an ecumenical shared parish is its members' radical commitment to each other. In their daily living, they demonstrate trust in the spiritual journey and a certainty that they are being led by the Spirit into a new venture, one that looks and feels different from anything they have known before. Parishioners at Spirit of Grace Lutheran-Episcopal Church in West Bloomfield expressed the grace and deepened sense of God's guidance that they have found through the federation process at their parish. "We do not have a clue where God is going to take us," one member said. "But we have to be willing to go and not stay where we are. If we stay where we are, we are going to die; we will perish. I do not have a clue at this point in time what God is calling us to do, but we have got to totally die to self and be willing to trust completely in God and say: 'Take us where You will and we will be here to follow.'"[26] And Father Lucas of the Church of the Nativity and

25. Spirit of Grace, West Bloomfield, Van Blarcum, interview.
26. Spirit of Grace, West Bloomfield, Campbell, interview.

Holy Comforter in Baltimore said, "I can't tell you how exciting this is. Every day is different."[27]

27. Church of the Nativity and Holy Comforter, Lucas, interview with the Lutheran Episcopal Coordinating Committee of the Metropolitan Washington, DC Synod, Diocese of Washington and Diocese of Virginia.

2

Two Traditions Forging Partnership

Debts/trespasses. Kneeling hassocks/communion cup holders. Bright, colonial-styled worship space/processional cross. Common chalice/table. Alb/Geneva gown. Presbytery/Diocese. Bishop/Executive Presbyter. Historic Episcopate/Representative leadership. These contrasts are Rubicons great and small to be crossed when Episcopalians and Presbyterians—or churches holding these polities—inhabit one congregation together. Indian Hill Episcopal-Presbyterian Church in Cincinnati represents a successful example of such cooperation.

Surrounded by lovely homes and adjacent to a country club, this church's affluence may be its most apparent demographic feature, but it is not its most important one. It has been a shared ministry since 1931, with roots as a lay-organized neighborhood Sunday school and later a congregation jointly sponsored by presbytery and diocese. The church is both a parish of the Diocese of Southern Ohio and a congregation of the Cincinnati Presbytery, and it maintains separate membership rosters, though parishioners rarely wear one affiliation on their sleeves. Many simply consider themselves members of Indian Hill and make little of one or another of the traditions. Yet tradition matters here, and members reject the "community church" or "interdenominational" label even as they carry Episcopalian or Presbyterian affiliations lightly. There is a concerted effort to take both heritages seriously. Magnanimous openness to one another and to anyone who finds the church attractive is the order of things at Indian Hill.

Congregations such as Indian Hill, who belong to two traditions, but whose sponsoring denominations are not in full communion, liberally dot the

American landscape. They represent over half of the ecumenical parishes in Canada, many of which are Anglican/United Church of Canada shared ministries. Although few are as old as Indian Hill, many of them pre-date the full communion conversations and processes of the late twentieth century. Some, like Indian Hill and parishes created in the 1960s and 1970s in the resource towns of the Canadian north, began as ecumenical projects, but more were mergers of existing congregations. They comprise pairings of many traditions: Anglican (Canada), Baptist, Christian Church (Disciples of Christ), Episcopalian (USA), Lutheran, Mennonite, Presbyterian, United Church of Canada, and United Methodist. (For shared ministries with Roman Catholic partners, see chapter 4).

Each of these shared parishes navigates its way uniquely, with its own story to tell. Underlying all of them, however, is the desire and commitment to live and worship together. "We intend to stay together," the World Council of Churches announced at its founding meeting in 1948, and these congregations echo that sentiment. They pledge and work to stay together, despite challenges from within and without. Shared ministries outside of full communion partnerships are rather like couples who fall in love across differing cultural backgrounds. Not only does the couple have cultural issues to settle with each other, their parents may not be entirely sold on the viability of the relationship. Yet, these congregations persist—and have done so for decades, in some cases.

In this chapter, we meet some congregations that share denominational identities outside of full communion agreements. We hear their founding stories. We learn how they have learned to work out their theological, liturgical, and governance differences, and how they weather the challenges that emerge in their life together.

How do these sharing arrangements arise? What prompts Episcopalians to kneel beside pew-sitting Presbyterians? Their origins are as varied as their traditions and locations. Here are a few of their stories:

INDIAN HILL CHURCH (EPISCOPAL-PRESBYTERIAN), CINCINNATI

The Indian Hill congregation began as a cooperative Sunday school for children in the private neighborhood home of a Presbyterian woman in the early 1930s. However, this cooperation developed into shared worship and ministry.

"The primary foundational concept," the congregation states, "was to provide a local church that would meet the needs of Episcopalians and Presbyterians living in the Indian Hill area, and to do so intentionally as an experiment in ecumenicity."[1] It is not clear, however, whether the idea for a federated congregation was a natural development of the grassroots effort or the result of promptings by the ecumenically minded Bishop Henry Hobson of the Diocese of Southern Ohio. Hobson had promoted rapprochement between Episcopalians and Presbyterians on the national level, and it is quite possible he saw in Indian Hill a kind of prototype for federated congregations of the two traditions. Local memory suggests that the story of a Presbyterian laywoman offering Christian education to Episcopal youngsters in her home intrigued the local bishop. Clergy from both downtown Cincinnati churches had been alternating visits to Indian Hill homes to lead worship services. Whatever the source, Indian Hill was on its way to a unique history in a neighborhood populated by the captains of Cincinnati industry and commerce.[2]

The federated congregations called an Episcopalian, the Rev. Luther Tucker, in 1949 for what would be a twenty-four-year ministry. Tucker was perhaps the perfect combination of patrician and ecumenist, a veteran of campus ministry at Yale University and an associate of the World Student Christian Federation. A succession of Presbyterian co-pastors joined Fr. Tucker, including, for a time, a third pastor for youth work. Among the first shared tasks was the construction of a church, a simple stone and slate-roofed building modeled after examples in New England. The wealthy congregation paid for the structure before its completion in 1952.[3]

What do the present clergy and members say about the strengths of this church? "What makes it work is equal sharing, especially by the clergy," said one member. "Any problems we've had stem from that—either abrogating or dominating."[4] It takes a Presbyterian minister and an Episcopal priest enthusiastic about ecumenism and able to work together; who recognize the validity of both traditions. Nearly seventy years later, the ecumenical partnership continues.

1. Indian Hill Church, "Our History."
2. Long, *Indian Hill Church Blue Book History*.
3. Long, *Indian Hill Church Blue Book History*, 17.
4. Indian Hill Church, Cincinnati, group interview.

ST. PAUL'S INTERNATIONAL PASTORAL CHARGE, NORTH DAKOTA/SASKATCHEWAN

Why simply cross denominational lines to form a shared ministry when you can also cross an international border? That is what occurred when rural Presbyterians in northernmost North Dakota, and rural United Church members in southernmost Saskatchewan formed an international pastoral charge in 1965. Here is how one member, Kay Wilson, tells the story: "By 1964, it was patently obvious that some of our small congregations in the area were doomed to disappear. . . . Fewer people were coming to worship on Sunday, and the coffers were strained. After many meetings (an oversimplification of the work done), the International Pastoral Charge was born."[5]

Since 1966, the congregations of Knox United, North Portal (Saskatchewan) and First Presbyterian, Portal (North Dakota), have worshiped together, one month on the American side of the border and one month on the Canadian side. They have been served by both United Church of Canada and American Presbyterian clergy. (In 2005, they united with another United Church, St. Paul's, Estevan, but continue their monthly cross-border Sunday worship.) "We have much in common," writes Kay Wilson: "We are all prairie people. We worry about the same things: our families, our crops, our world neighbors. The Canadian meets the American at the door after church and says, 'Great day, eh?' And the American replies, 'You bet! That was quite a rain, huh!' . . . Only the 'ehs' and the 'huhs' tell us apart. We are privileged to worship in this 'hands across the border' setting."[6]

BROADWAY DISCIPLES UNITED, WINNIPEG

Downtown Winnipeg, Manitoba, is the setting for another kind of border-crossing: Broadway Disciples United represents the merger of a Disciples of Christ congregation made up largely of Filipino Canadians with two United Church congregations: one small and Filipino, the other larger, mostly Caucasian. The impetus came from the Disciples minister, the Rev. Ray Cuthbert, who saw in the late 1990s that his congregation, Home St. Christian Church, worshiping in a rented building on a side street, needed a challenge. Cuthbert, who had been formed in Disciples of Christ ecumenism, and without other Disciples congregations in Winnipeg, readily looked to other traditions for

5. Wilson, "Shared Ministry with an International Flavour: The International (Saskatchewan and North Dakota) Pastoral Charge," in Barker, *Lively Option*, 63.

6. Wilson, "Shared Ministry with an International Flavour: The International (Saskatchewan and North Dakota) Pastoral Charge," in Barker, *Lively Option*, 65.

partners. He knew the tiny Filipino United Church, renting space in another church's building, needed a home. St. Stephen's Broadway United, a piece of prime downtown real estate, had been for sale for a year. Although still financially viable, the congregation's members were old and tired, and its membership was in decline. The sale was in the hands of the United Church presbytery. The asking price was one million dollars. Cuthbert contacted the presbytery chairperson, the Rev. Eleanor Geib. "Well, Ray," she said, "that congregation's really ready to go. Couldn't we just let them die?"

The only way to have a conversation with the congregation was to offer to buy the building. The Home Street board wrote a letter indicating their interest in the church—but admitting they had no money. It was enough to open the conversation. The three congregations decided to rotate worship in each other's spaces for a while. However, a mere few weeks later they held a joint Palm Sunday service in the large downtown church, and they fell in love. They agreed to live together for six months, as a trial. They abolished the committees of all three congregations, formed three new committees (worship, pastoral care, administration/finance), and appointed three members from each congregation to each.

"So we did that," Cuthbert explained, "and the people who were the most enthusiastic were the St. Stephen's Broadway folks. To them it was like new life had been breathed into them." This new life came in no small measure from the infusion of young immigrant Filipinos. "I can still hear the St. Stephen's voices. They were saying, 'There are children here again!' The little kids were happy because they inherited all these grandparents. We had everyone wear name tags. . . . Within three months, everybody knew: this was it." They formally constituted the shared ministry in 1998. Moreover, one of their greatest cheerleaders was Eleanor Geib, the United Church Presbytery chair.[7]

Like other ecumenical parishes, non-full communion congregations emerge in a variety of contexts. What their founding stories hold in common is the willingness to cross borders and boundaries to seek partnership. Someone, or some group of people, thought "outside the box" of their own denomination—and perhaps of their own nation and culture—to imagine a relationship that others might not have considered. Who are these "someones"? They might be neighbors chatting "over the fence" about their churches' lives and needs. They could be clergy who become friends across denominations and envision a common ministry. They may be individuals who have been formed ecumenically or who have a gift for seeing possibilities beyond the expected norms. They may be church leaders, anticipating a deeper ecumenical future for their denominations. However the inspiration emerges, this ecumenical

7. Broadway Disciples United, Cuthbert interview.

creativity must be accompanied by the determination to show everyone involved—congregants, judicatories, and the community—these unconventional partnerships are more than possibilities—they are life giving.

So why bother? Why not just go it alone, or amalgamate with the closest parish of one's own denomination? As the stories above point out, the resources often do not exist to begin or continue in ministry "alone," and there may be no obvious nearby parish of the same denomination with whom to amalgamate. However, the desire for ecumenical partnership may reach even deeper than financial need and geographic proximity. Sometimes, as in the case of Indian Hill, the two groups share a pre-existing ministry and mission, and judicatory leaders who carry an ecumenical vision. Sometimes, as happened with a United Church of Canada congregation that needed to find a new home in uptown Toronto, a shared ministry allows a congregation to *preserve* its identity. When Deer Park United Church formed a shared worshiping community with the local Presbyterian congregation, the United Church parish maintained its name, its relationship with the ecumenical "Churches on the Hill" group it had helped to instigate, and other aspects of its uniqueness. On the other hand, a same-denomination amalgamation likely "would have meant the end of Deer Park."[8] In that strange way the Gospel has of turning the world upside down, ecumenical shared parishes offer the opportunity to "lose one's life" only to find it in a new way.

WORKING OUT THE DIFFERENCES

Once two ecumenical partners have found one another, they need to determine how they will live together, and to formalize that relationship. It rarely happens quickly. Even if the congregations bond faster than they might have imagined, as they did at Broadway Disciples United, the work of forming the covenant takes time and patience. They need to figure out not only what they have in common, but also what makes each partner distinct, and how they will respect those distinctions. This attention to honoring the gifts of both traditions sets ecumenical shared ministries apart from "non-denominational" or "community" churches. It is not the case that tradition does not matter. Rather, *both* traditions matter. How they account for all that matters makes them the unique entities they are. While other chapters in this book delve more deeply into covenant formation, worship, and governance, let us observe how some of these non-full communion congregations navigate those waters.

8. Deer Park and Calvin, Goodyear, interview.

Ministry

Clergy in non-full communion shared ministries face special challenges and vulnerabilities. Because the sharing congregations generally do not have the backing of an interdenominational "mutual recognition of ministries" agreement, they rely on the congregational covenant or constitution, and the support and good will of both the congregation and the participating judicatories, to authorize and sustain their work. At the official level, both denominations need to recognize the legitimacy of the serving clergyperson in some way, such as through a bishop's license, or a denominational motion or letter of appointment. Everyone involved must be clear about what ministry functions clergyperson is "permitted" to exercise. In Canada, for example, some Anglican bishops allow United Church or Presbyterian clergy to celebrate the Eucharist using Anglican rites, but others do not. Making these details plain is crucial at the start of a new pastorate.

Of course, more complex are the unofficial expectations of the clergy relationship. Competent and seasoned pastors may suddenly find themselves on a sharp learning curve. A willingness to learn and to "let go" are common themes among shared ministry clergy. "Get ready to let go of your certainty about how to do things," said Leigh Sinclair, a United Church of Canada minister who has served two interchurch congregations: "You need to let go of what you know is right, and embrace what makes people reach for God."[9] Or, as Marie Goodyear, the United Church minister at Calvin Presbyterian/Deer Park United Church, put it: "You have to respect everything, even if you think it's trivial. And you have to be able to laugh hysterically when you need to, and you also have to know how not to take yourself too seriously, and not vest yourself too much in stuff."[10] Asking for grace and forgiveness is also key for clergy. As Barbara Martin, an Anglican priest serving an Anglican/United Church, wrote in the annual parish report, "Becoming familiar with the United Church has been a mental challenge. I am three-quarters of the way home on this, but the final quarter will be the toughest. I thank you for your understanding and support."[11]

Where understanding and support are lacking, the resulting conflict can be complicated in non-full communion shared ministries. Sometimes the conflict relates directly to the ecumenical sharing. A Canadian Anglican priest in the 1970s loved being in ecumenical shared ministry so much that he served more than one shared parish, and even wrote a small memoir of his

9. St. Peter's Ecumenical Church, Sinclair, interview.

10. Deer Park and Calvin, Goodyear, interview.

11. St. Paul's-St. Cuthbert's Church, Princeton, Annual Report, 1981.

adventures. Yet, when he left his second parish, the United Church members asked to terminate the sharing agreement. Why? In their experience, what the Anglican cleric really "loved" was imposing Anglican traditions on them.[12] However, in shared ministry any kind of conflict can be attributed to a perceived failure of the ecumenical sharing. If the congregation and its judicatories are not firm in their commitment to ecumenical cooperation, leaders can use conflict with one clergyperson as "evidence" that the sharing agreement is flawed or should even be terminated. We have seen examples of congregations and judicatories who have terminated shared ministries agreements based on conflict with one clergyperson.[13]

On the other hand, shared congregations that are mature and firm in their relationship can weather conflict between clergy and congregants. The Indian Hill congregation and its clergy were deeply committed to race relations work in Cincinnati. The first Presbyterian co-pastor at Indian Hill was the Rev. Wilhelmina Rowland, who went on to a career in Christian Education administration and civil rights work. The Rev. Paul Long and others extended that work. As we have noted, Indian Hill hired a succession of third ministers in addition to founding minister Tucker and Long, to oversee youth work. The first was popular among disenfranchised young people seeking voice to their opposition to the Vietnam War and their rejection of materialism. This made him unpopular with their parents. His successor failed in the opposite way, giving voice to parental concerns while losing the favor of the youth. Ecumenism, per se, was not the obstacle. The Indian Hill church recognized this reality, and the shared ministry survived.

The demands on clergy of non-full communion shared ministries can be tough, but the rewards are equally impressive. There is delight in learning new ways of ministering, and in helping congregations to love across boundaries. "It has made me more patient and more impatient. I am more patient with differences; I have to live 'God loves everybody' every day. I have to figure out not only how to love them, but how to honor them. . . . But I am impatient with my own denomination and what I now see is its narrowness," said Leigh Sinclair.[14] "Whatever difficulties I list," Ray Cuthbert reflects, "they are in the shadow of living my life's dream. Because I believe that Christ has one church on earth and any footstep toward that is a good footstep. It is telling the world

---

12. Name withheld by mutual agreement, interview by Sandra Beardsall, March 20, 2012.

13. See, for example, Kamloops Okanagan Presbytery Minutes, 1981+: Jan. 11, 1982, April 26, 1982.

14. St. Peter's Ecumenical Church, Sinclair, interview.

that we are about Christ and not about a denominational shingle. All of that has been a dream come true."[15]

Worship

Decisions around worship in a shared ministry can be as subtle as deciding whether to use "debts" or "trespasses" in the Lord's Prayer, or as obvious as the structure of the Eucharistic liturgy. Even when the two traditions share much in common, it is important to think through the ways worship will unfold. At The Brandermill Church, a Presbyterian/United Methodist shared parish in Virginia, the Sunday worship service is conventionally mainline Protestant. Pastors vest in pulpit gowns and stoles. The Brandermill congregation makes choices about those few real differences between how Presbyterians and United Methodists usually worship: congregants pray the Lord's Prayer, saying "debts and debtors," typically Reformed practice. Communion reception practice has varied among pew (Presbyterian), altar rail (Methodist), intinction, and individual cup. At Brandermill, the hymnals are labeled "Brandermill Church Hymnal" with an outline of the building embossed on the cover. They are, in fact, the 1989 United Methodist Hymnal. When the sharing traditions develop their own liturgy in this way, weaving the elements of both traditions into their weekly pattern, the resulting worship tends to take the name "blended" or "hybrid." (See chapter 7 for a further discussion of worship patterns.)

When the liturgical differences are more striking, the consultation becomes more rigorous. Some elements are not negotiable: Disciples of Christ celebrate the Lord's Supper weekly, so the United Church agreed to participate in weekly communion. As the Anglican/Episcopal Eucharistic rite requires a celebrant whom the bishop has licensed, this becomes a complicating factor in any non-full communion ministry with an Anglican/Episcopalian partner. Where a congregation has two (or more) clergy, one of each denomination, they can model unity in the liturgy. At Indian Hill Church, the clergy participate in both Sunday morning services, the 8:00 Episcopal Holy Eucharist and the 10:30 Presbyterian service. Flexibility and unity without violation of the integrity of either tradition is the standard. Therefore, both clergy co-officiate at each service.

Where there is only one ministry staff person, however, the congregation must develop its own pattern. Many rotate denominational services weekly, using an agreed-upon pattern of Morning Prayer and communion services. Where necessary, shared ministries make room for a guest Anglican/

15. Broadway Disciples United, Cuthbert, interview.

Episcopalian Eucharistic celebrant in the rota. Some non-full communion shared ministries with more disparate worship traditions have also developed blended liturgies, such as the Evangelical Lutheran Church in Canada/United Church of Canada congregations of Shell Lake ("Partners in Worship") and Spiritwood (Trinity Bissell Memorial Church), both in Saskatchewan.

These negotiations do not produce simply a liturgical compromise. Rather, participants in ecumenically shared congregations describe a deepening of their worship experience. For example, though the Rev. Heather Wiseman of Indian Hill prefers the Episcopalian manner of receiving the Eucharist, she has learned to appreciate the Presbyterian manner of elders sent forth from the table to the pews with the elements, comparing it to Jesus sending out the apostles with the good news. However, the Episcopal service illustrates for her a complementary theme, namely, the call to grace in the invitation to come forward to receive the elements.[16] However, the Episcopal service illustrates for her a complementary theme, namely, the call to grace in the invitation to come forward to receive the elements. The Presbyterian minister at Indian Hill, Stephen Caine, speaks of the powerful sense of "home" that the *Book of Common Prayer* affords Episcopalians wherever they go in the world.[17]

Shared worship also affects the content of prayers and sermons. A Lutheran pastor who served in an Evangelical Lutheran/United Church of Canada shared ministry comments that this context pushed him to preach more biblically, as he could not assume a shared doctrinal identity.[18] Intercessory prayers in shared congregations expand to include the prayer cycles of the two denominations involved, testimony to the expanded horizons that mark the shared ministry experience.

Governance

Putting together the formal agreement, or covenant, for shared ministries not in full communion is an opportunity for simultaneous consternation and creativity. It is one thing to rejoice in each other's company and Christian fellowship; it is another thing to capture that shared spirit in the more judicial language required of the formal sharing agreement. The cooperation of judicatories in the preparation of the agreement, whether they are supportive or suspicious of the arrangement, is crucial for long-term survival. Moreover, while each ministry must carve its own path, using the templates and guidelines of

16. Indian Hill Church, interview.

17. Indian Hill Church, Cincinnati, interview.

18. Anonymous comment posted on ESM Survey, October 2011.

other ecumenically shared congregations can help avoid gaps and pitfalls. The challenge lies in making sure the structures represent the disparate polities of the denominations, without over-governing the congregation and exhausting the lay and ordered leaders. Indian Hill Church honors its Episcopalian/Presbyterian traditions through governance by a "Vestry Session." Members of the Vestry elect a Senior and Junior Warden annually, and members of the Session elect a Clerk and an Assistant Clerk annually. These four individuals make up the Advisory Committee, which meets monthly with both clergy and prepares the agenda for each month's meeting.

The Brandermill Church's agreement offers another example of careful construction. Like its worship, Brandermill's covenant has blended the two traditions in some places, has honored one or the other where appropriate, or, has established local practices that are amenable to both but originate with neither. This pragmatic approach might suggest Brandermill shares certain features commonly found in inter- or non-denominational churches, but members insist—and the covenant outlines—that their denominational traditions matter. In fact, one couple from a non-denominational church began attending Brandermill and were specifically impressed with the level of attention given to specific traditions, something they reported missing in their former church.[19]

Like all ecumenical shared ministry congregations, non-full communion partnerships need to stay in communication with their sponsoring denominations, through lay and clergy representation. For non-full communion ministries, however, the stakes are higher. This participation reminds the denominations that the congregation takes its dual nature seriously. Clergy often find the duplication of judicatories exhausting, and sometimes frustrating, if they appear anomalous, and are not allowed the "voice and vote" of their peers. However, attending meetings beyond those of one's denomination lends legitimacy to the sharing relationship. "The wider church work requires a lot of time and a lot of engagement. But if you don't do it, you have a harder time laying claim to the ecumenical vision,"[20] Ray Cuthbert said.

Non-full communion shared ministries can fall prey to the vagaries of individual denominational leaders and their attitudes toward ecumenism. While this can occur in any interchurch ministry, without the overarching commitments of an interdenominational agreement, shared ministries become more vulnerable. The failure of the church union plan between the Anglicans and United Church in Canada in the mid-1970s, and the appointment of a new bishop, left the many shared ministries in the Kootenay diocese in a

19. Brandermill Church, group interview.
20. Broadway Disciples United, Cuthbert, interview.

precarious position. The bishop uncoupled several sharing arrangements, and made clear that he was unconvinced about the need for others. At one point, in frustration, a United Church lay representative to Kootenay Presbytery from a shared ministry expostulated, for the record: "We are fulfilling God's purpose. The problem is with the hierarchy."[21]

Two decades later, the Evangelical Lutheran bishop of Alberta and the Territories wrote a pastoral letter to the congregations of his synod in response to some theological remarks made by the United Church of Canada Moderator in an interview with an Ottawa newspaper. "We will review on a case by case basis each shared ministry we engage in to ensure that no member of our church involved in such a shared ministry will have to wonder if they in good conscience can continue that involvement because of theological concerns."[22] It is not clear that such an investigation occurred. However, the alarm such remarks can cause to shared ministries is palpable.

IS IT WORTH IT?

Given the challenges and the vulnerabilities that can imperil non-full communion shared ministries, is it all worth the bother? Indian Hill and Brandermill would not turn back. Nor would the Anglican/United Church Windermere Valley Shared Ministry in British Columbia, celebrating fifty years and still going strong. Perhaps the most rewarding aspect for those who undertake such ministry is that it is a daring plunge into a future known only to God. Said Marie Goodyear of Deer Park United and Calvin Presbyterian:

> I am positive about this: even if people are opposed to any kind of shared ministry, especially ecumenical shared ministry, if you give it a chance, you find things in it that you never would have expected. . . . I could have ended my ministry by saying: "Well, we closed, and I retired," and instead, I get to end my ministry on a high.[23]

Awit Marcelino, a young lay leader at Broadway Disciples United agreed: "If you want your church to have new life, there is an alternative. We struggled for a long time, but it is worth it. It can be a different path, different than what you wanted it to be, but it may be what God wants it to be."[24] Ray Cuthbert echoes her sentiment: "Nearly half a century ago, J. B. Phillips said, 'Your God

21. Kootenay Presbytery Minutes, Oct. 17–19, 1976.

22. Stephen P. Kristenson, "To the Congregations of the Synod," Nov. 28, 1997.

23. Deer Park and Calvin, Goodyear, interview.

24. Broadway Disciples United, Marcelino, interview.

is too small,' and it's a pretty good slogan for ecumenical shared ministries. When we really realize this is about God and not about us . . . we realize there is something here that is about more than just us."[25]

25. Broadway Disciples United, Cuthbert, interview.

3

Crossing the Protestant-Roman Catholic Boundary

ECUMENICAL SHARED PARISHES OF every stripe are communities of hope and expectation, but none more than those few that are successfully bridging the Protestant-Catholic divide. The Second Vatican Council (1962–65) propelled the Roman Catholic Church into ecumenical relations with Protestants. The church entered almost immediately into bilateral dialogues with the Lutheran World Federation in 1967 and with the Anglican Communion in 1970. Yet the reality on the ground was almost total separation, even in interdenominational families. In a personal email to one of the authors, a Catholic layperson mused, "I could never understand why, in my tradition or in God's eyes, something was vitally wrong with my loving, caring Lutheran relatives. I would find it a delight to be able to transport myself back and tell my Lutheran uncles, aunts, and cousins how much I love them for the virtue their faith tradition brought them. We reverenced one another, but it was not an era of dialogue nor intermingling as it is at least in some areas today." This was the lived experience of denominational separation before the accomplishments of the ecumenical movement of the late twentieth and early twenty-first centuries.

In the excitement and fervor of the early days of ecumenism, many Catholics, Anglicans, Lutherans, and other Protestants hoped and expected that these Christian communions would soon unite. Out of this hope emerged ecumenical parish ventures in the United States and Canada. In parts of Canada, Catholics and non-Catholics began to share worship spaces, youth work, and other ministries. On Vancouver Island, the sharing took a deeper turn as the Roman Catholic and Anglican bishops, together with United Church presbytery and conference personnel, cooperated wherever possible, including shared worship. One community at the north end of Vancouver Island developed a Eucharistic liturgy, approved by all three denominations, which they celebrated together. We describe the Port Alice Liturgy in more detail in chapter 7.

Meanwhile, in the United States, two novel ecumenical congregational ventures were launched on opposite sides of the country. In Virginia Beach, the Episcopal Diocese of Southern Virginia and the Roman Catholic Diocese of Richmond launched the Church of the Holy Apostles in 1977. "At the time the formation for the preparation of the parish was going on," recalled one member, "it was thought that it would only be five years before the two churches would reunite."[1] Inspired in part by the Church of the Holy Apostles, the Mission of the Atonement: A Community of Roman Catholics and Lutherans, was established in Beaverton, Oregon eight years later.

These two parishes have gone boldly beyond denominational boundaries to forge new ground as ecumenical parishes, while remaining rooted in their dual denominational identities. They are living laboratories of the Lund principle, which states that churches should work together in everything except where conviction requires them to act separately. These parishes are arguably the greatest innovators of the ministries covered in this book. This chapter looks at why these congregations were formed, how they survive and thrive, how they have the tenacity to continue, and how they deal with changing judicatories.

"CHOOSING LOVE OVER SEPARATION": CHURCH OF THE HOLY APOSTLES, VIRGINIA BEACH

Founding Story

The Church of the Holy Apostles in Virginia Beach is the only Episcopal-Roman Catholic shared parish in the country. The idea began in an after-dinner conversation between Bishop Walter Sullivan of the Roman Catholic Diocese of Richmond and Bishop David Rose of the Episcopal Diocese of Southern Virginia, church leaders who shared a forward-looking ecumenical vision, and who also sought to serve the many Episcopal-Roman Catholic mixed marriages in the Virginia Beach area. It was to be a foretaste of

---

1. Church of the Holy Apostles, Pollie, interview.

soon-to-be-forthcoming (or so it was thought) Anglican-Roman Catholic full communion unity.

A joint committee of five Episcopalians and five Roman Catholics was appointed in 1975 to explore the idea and to design a proposal for this shared parish. The joint committee envisioned Holy Apostles as a "visible sign of Christian unity . . . eucharistically centered, intent on mission, involved in shared ministry, creative in liturgy, expressive in total stewardship, committed to Christian education and formation, ecumenically optimistic."[2] The parish was established with the installation of Episcopal and Roman Catholic co-pastors on November 1, 1977, followed by the first liturgy on December 4, 1977.

The preamble of the Holy Apostles' Constitution, adopted in June 1978, provides a theological statement of the members' commitment to this venture:

> We, the people of the Church of the Holy Apostles, united by our faith in Jesus Christ; distinctive in our historical traditions; seeking to deepen our own faith lives, and thus helping to heal the wounds which separate one Christian body from another; striving to minister to each other and to persons in our surrounding civic and ecclesial communities; working for the establishment of peace and justice; proclaiming and advocating efforts at ecumenical action; aware that our Congregation, duly instituted by the Episcopal diocese of Southern Virginia and the Roman Catholic diocese of Richmond, is the first Anglican/Roman Catholic foundation in the United States, do ordain and establish this Constitution.[3]

This inaugural description still holds true of the people and clergy of this parish nearly forty years later. An encounter with this Christian community today reveals that they are still united yet distinctive in their traditions, spiritually mature, pastorally sensitive, committed to peace, justice, and ecumenical action, and a strong community of faith and witness to the gospel in the community of Virginia Beach and beyond.

Working Out the Logistics

Initially this start-up was dependent upon mission funding from the two founding dioceses. In February 1983, it became a self-supporting congregation. The parish has one budget, one governing body, and a unified administrative policy. Expenses are shared equally. The membership has historically

2. Church of the Holy Apostles, *Parish Profile*, 1.
3. Constitution of the Anglican/Roman Catholic Church of the Holy Apostles.

been about one-third Episcopal, two-thirds Catholic, but the apportionment finances have always been divided 50/50 between the Roman Catholic diocese and the Episcopal diocese. There is one budget and one stewardship drive. At first, every parish committee was constituted with Roman Catholic and Episcopal co-chairs and representative committee membership. That strict division eased over time as members came to view themselves as unified members of Holy Apostles first and foremost, and Roman Catholics or Episcopalians second.

Ministry and Membership

From 1977 to 2011, the parish was served by Roman Catholic and Episcopal priests who functioned as co-pastors in every way. They were each to consider themselves ministers to all members of the parish and to serve as equals in all aspects of parish life and ministry, providing pastoral oversight, sacramental ministry, program coordination, and ecumenical direction, as well as oversight over the use of the building and the design for worship. The collaboration between the co-pastors, the respective bishops, and the laity of the parish has been the glue for this congregation for nearly forty years. Since 2012, the Roman Catholic leadership has consisted of a half-time deacon and a chaplain/priest for Sunday services, serving in partnership with a full-time Episcopal priest.

About one-third of the parish membership is made up of Episcopal-Catholic mixed marriages and families. The congregation also includes some Catholic-Lutheran and Catholic-Baptist ecumenical families. Long-term member Lee Startt bore witness to the importance of this ecumenical parish for his family life. "I grew up [Catholic] and married an Episcopalian so I think I can speak with some authority on ecumenism. I have been living it all my life. I think that Holy Apostles is the answer to all my prayers when it comes to ecumenism. It has enabled me not to split my family on Sunday morning for the last thirty-eight years. I raised two children who are faith-filled grownups and who are raising their children the same way. Ecumenism worked!"[4]

How Worship Works

The Parish Profile drawn up in 1991 for the search for a new Episcopal priest described Holy Apostles' principle of worship in this way: "Our biggest challenge has been combining the two traditions without compromising either. . . .

4. Church of the Holy Apostles, Lee Startt, interview.

This has often been manifested by combining when allowable, duplicating when needed, and separating when required."[5] The story of worship practice here is complex. The parish has journeyed through various phases of Eucharistic worship, always trying to honor the sensibilities of both traditions while also seeking to share as much as they possibly could. And they have at times pushed forward with sound ecumenical innovation to make the unity that they share in Christ visible in their worship practices.

This is a story of the interplay of liturgy, architecture, and, most of all, the love of a close-knit parish called to unity. At the beginning, the Eucharist was celebrated in separate buildings with a lay member "often taking the bread and wine through the rain or snow from the main building to the Communion site."[6] Later, the nave was modified to accommodate a main altar at the front and another altar under the choir loft. The Catholic and Episcopal priests alternated use of those altars and celebrating the Eucharist in both traditions simultaneously, each priest using the Eucharistic blessing of their own tradition. This was so groundbreaking that *Time Magazine* published an article about it in February 1981.[7] "When it came time for the Lord's Prayer," said member Joan Flowers, "everybody stretched out and around the whole rim of the church, held hands and said the Lord's Prayer."[8] Another member recalled that the gathering and joining hands happened for the first time at the Easter Vigil in 1978. "It sort of happened spontaneously," he said. "The Catholics gathered at one end for their Eucharist, [Episcopalians] at the opposite, and when the Lord's Prayer came up in the liturgy, we just sort of spontaneously stretched out and made a circle around the entire church, and there were literally tears in people's eyes, at the symbolism of that."[9]

In these early years, worship music was an issue, with unfamiliar hymnody from the different traditions, so for a while, the church alternated between Catholic chant and Episcopal contemporary music. Eventually the congregation came to accept, and even love, each other's hymnody. As Don and Emily Saliers describe in their book, *A Song to Sing, a Life to Live*, learning to love one another's music creates relationship and connection, and, ultimately, love between each other.[10]

The parish's early worship design, which they called a Para-Liturgy, began in early 1978. It provided a unified welcome and opening prayers and

5. Church of the Holy Apostles, *Parish Profile*, 12.

6. Church of the Holy Apostles, *First Ten Years*, 1.

7. "Religion: Two Altars, One Mass."

8. Church of the Holy Apostles, Flowers, interview.

9. Church of the Holy Apostles, Startt, interview.

10. Saliers and Saliers, *Song to Sing*, 112–14.

then a "Pilgrimage" of one of the groups (Episcopalians and Roman Catholics alternating weekly) to a neighboring classroom for separate liturgies of the Word and of the Eucharist.[11] The practice of two altars in the nave of the sanctuary was re-established sometime after the parish moved into the current church building in 1985. With an altar at either end of the nave, the congregation shared the service of the Word as a united body, then moved to their respective altars for the Eucharist. Initially, the Eucharistic prayers were offered simultaneously: Episcopal at one altar, Catholic at the other. Then they finished the service together and shared the post-Communion prayer and the final blessing. This shared worship pattern at Holy Apostles continued without disruption for more than two more decades.

The next phase of the parish's worship life came as an abrupt surprise to the clergy and members of the parish. A Roman Catholic layperson from Florida, Charles J. Cassini, had attended worship at Holy Apostles while traveling through Virginia Beach. He subsequently published an article about his experience at Holy Apostles, entitled "Why Eucharistic Sharing must WAIT," in the June 19, 2011 issue of *The Living Church*, an Episcopal news magazine. Himself part of a mixed marriage—his wife is an Episcopal priest—Cassini wrote the article in a laudatory tone. However, its descriptions of worship at Holy Apostles sparked a reader of the article to lodge a formal complaint with the Apostolic Nunciature in Washington, DC. The matter then went to Rome, where it was brought to the attention of the Roman Catholic Bishop of the Diocese of Richmond, Bishop Francis DiLorenzo.

In response to the concerns raised about shared worship at Holy Apostles, the Episcopal and Roman Catholic priests who serve the parish wrote a letter to the editor of *The Living Church* to clarify the parish's worship practice. They noted their parish was using a "blended Eucharistic prayer that merges salient portions of Eucharistic Prayer B (Rite II) from the [Episcopal] *Book of Common Prayer* and Eucharistic Prayers II, III, and IV from the Roman Catholic Sacramentary." Between the *Sursum corda* and the Words of Institution, and between the Words of Institution and the Doxology, where the prayers differ, the celebrants would alternate, paragraph by paragraph. "The Words of Institution and Doxology are identical and are, therefore, spoken in unison," they explained. "We do truly believe that the model that has evolved at Holy Apostles could provide a way of sharing those portions of our two traditions while allowing both traditions to remain separate in those aspects on which complete accord has yet to be achieved."[12] A teenager who grew up in the parish said that shared worship seems normal to him, "When I go to another

11. Church of the Holy Apostles, *First Ten Years*, 7.

12. Ferguson and Parke, "Celebrating Together," 27.

Catholic church or with my grandfather, I am [thinking], 'Wait—where are the two altars?' I am used to the unique traditions that we do here. I am drawn in by Holy Apostles' uniqueness."[13]

The Roman Catholic bishop, however, found the parish's worship pattern unsatisfactory. By Advent 2012, he removed the Roman Catholic priest of Holy Apostles, Fr. James Parke, co-signer of the letter to the editor. The bishop also insisted that the parish move to two services, with the Roman Catholic and Episcopal liturgies completely separated from one another. Parishioners were upset over the unexpected removal of the Roman Catholic priest and over separate services after worshiping together as one congregation for so long. Those in mixed marriages were especially upset that the opportunity to worship as a family would end. The Episcopal priest serving the parish, the Rev. Michael Ferguson, worked with the Roman Catholic diocesan liturgist, seeking a solution or compromise that might be satisfactory to the bishop while maintaining the parish's long-standing tradition of shared worship. Ferguson was able to structure two sequential services that met the bishop's concerns and complied with the Catholic Church's norms, and the bishop appointed a Roman Catholic hospital chaplain to celebrate at the Catholic mass.

On Sunday, November 1, 2015, the parish's thirty-eighth anniversary, about 120 people gathered for worship. The services ran back-to-back, one immediately after the other. The Episcopal liturgy was held first, and at the closing recessional, the congregation stayed in place. A bell was rung, and the Roman Catholic service began immediately. The congregation stayed in place and participated in the second service also. At each Eucharist, all came forward: the Catholics receiving a blessing at the Episcopal Eucharist and the Episcopalians receiving a blessing at the Catholic Eucharist. Each worship service took about 45 minutes. Nearly everyone came for the first service and stayed for both services as an expression of their commitment to the shared ecumenical venture. A long-term member of Holy Apostles asserted, "I can honestly say I would rather be here than any other church that I know of. If it means a marathon on Sunday mornings and staying through two services, I will do that, but I am hoping someday that will change. I see a future for us; it is not coming fast enough. But I am hopeful."[14] She reflects the commitment on the part of the people of this parish to stay and to worship together.

After a period of alternating which worship service came first, the parish decided to start the Episcopal Eucharistic service at 10 a.m. with the Roman Catholic Mass immediately following. Signs were erected along the parkway to inform the community and welcome visitors. The reality of people's busy

13. Church of the Holy Apostles, Russo, interview.

14. Church of the Holy Apostles, Flowers, interview.

lives has meant that not all are willing or able to stay for the two successive services each week. The deacon reports that more people leave after the first service than come in for the second service. Non-Eucharistic joint prayer and worship opportunities, such as healing liturgies and Lessons and Carols, supplement the separated Sunday Eucharist.

Challenges Today—Clerical Leadership

The Episcopal priest, the Rev. Michael Ferguson, announced his impending retirement in early 2016. The parish was just beginning to think through future transition when Father Ferguson died unexpectedly of a heart attack in the summer. The Episcopal diocese appointed a half-time interim Episcopal co-pastor, the Rev. Alan Mead, while the Roman Catholic deacon, the Rev. Gary Harmeyer, provided continuity. Father Rene Castillo continued to offer Catholic mass on Sundays. At the time of writing, a Discernment Committee is working on the selection of a permanent Episcopal co-pastor.

Looking Toward the Future: The Hope for Survival, Even Flourishing

What will the future look like for the Church of the Holy Apostles? The first hope is the survival of this distinctive Episcopal-Catholic partnership. Second is the hope that they might someday return to a joint service, perhaps on the earlier model of a combined liturgy of the word, followed by contiguous, coordinated, yet separate Eucharistic liturgies. This would require the permission of the Roman Catholic hierarchy. Meanwhile, the parish waits for the opportunity to enjoy this liturgical practice again. Invitations just went out for the fortieth-anniversary celebration to be held on November 1, 2017, and parishioners hope the parish will continue as a symbol of Christian Unity for at least another forty years.

This journey over shared worship is emblematic of the identity questions at the heart of this parish. But the identity of Holy Apostles is much more than shared Sunday worship and ministry to interchurch families. This parish undertakes mission and outreach to the Virginia Beach community and beyond. It provides summer shelter to homeless families, displaced by high beach motel rates, and participates in feeding programs at the winter homeless shelter. They sell African goods to provide funds for wells in Africa and hold adult and baby diaper drives. In a church video posted on YouTube in 2013, Father Ferguson said, "We say here every Sunday that we think this is what God's calling us to be, and this is an opportunity that God has given us."[15] This is a parish living out its vision statement, day by day: "Choosing love over separation. Unity over division. Choosing Christ above all things."[16]

SHARING THE FAITH IN THE "LEAST RELIGIOUS" US CITY: MISSION OF THE ATONEMENT, BEAVERTON, OREGON

Founding Story

Spirit of Grace at Mission of the Atonement in Beaverton, Oregon is the only Lutheran-Roman Catholic shared parish in the United States. Located in a suburb of Portland, the church building was built in 1961 as a Lutheran parish affiliated with the American Lutheran Church. By 1985, debt struggles and a dwindling congregation threatened its survival. The Lutheran pastor connected with an auxiliary bishop of the Roman Catholic Archdiocese of Portland, who helped a large Roman Catholic parish in a nearby town to start a mission in Beaverton at the Lutheran church. In July 1986, the two groups began as a community planning to maintain separate identities. For insight and inspiration, several members visited the Church of the Holy Apostles Episcopal-Roman Catholic parish in Virginia Beach. Soon thereafter, the Beaverton arrangement evolved into a shared parish. As with Holy Apostles, they initially hoped that their two traditions (Roman Catholic and Lutheran) would reach a formal ecumenical agreement for full communion. However, today it remains a singular expression of unity between the two traditions.

Working Out the Logistics

From the beginning, the Catholic part of the ministry has held its official status with the Roman Catholic Archdiocese of Portland as a mission of St. Anthony's Catholic Church in Tigard. The Lutheran portion was originally affiliated with the Lutheran North Pacific District of the American Lutheran Church, now the Oregon Synod of the Evangelical Lutheran Church in America (ELCA).

15. Ferguson, "Shared Congregation Project."
16. Church of the Holy Apostles website.

The parish maintains separate Lutheran and Catholic councils, but most of the local church governance is handled in the combined congregational council. Worship, Christian education, and finances are handled jointly. Though the membership is roughly two-thirds Roman Catholic, congregational benevolence is divided equally between the two traditions.

The former pastor, the Rev. Dale Jamtgaard, described the design and development of Mission of the Atonement in a 1993 study guide for ecumenical reception, *Twelve Tales Untold*, in which he characterizes the parish's existence as a "miracle."[17] That miracle continues to deepen, and the congregation's home page offers this description of its identity today:

> Spirit of Grace is an intentional community of ELCA Lutherans, Roman Catholics, and other faith traditions worshiping and serving together at Mission of the Atonement. We affirm our welcome to all sexual orientations, gender identities, shapes, sizes, races, languages, faiths, and spiritual perspectives.
>
> · We believe that what unites us as Christians and children of one God is greater than the theological differences that separate us.
>
> · We believe we are called by Christ to be on this journey together.
>
> · We believe we often learn the most by listening.
>
> · We believe that we are called to attend to not just what Jesus died for, but what he lived for.
>
> · We believe centuries of misunderstandings and violence can be best undone by sitting and praying and living and serving the world side by side.
>
> · We believe that the best theologies emerge by the challenge of taking each other's stories seriously.
>
> · We believe, along with St. Augustine, that we haven't read the Bible correctly if it doesn't impel us to go out to love and serve our neighbor.
>
> · We believe that Jesus invites both personal transformation and cultural transformation—into God's peaceable kindom [*sic*] of non-violence, inclusion, healing, and wholeness.[18]

The parish has fostered positive relations with a succession of judicatory leaders as both denominations have experienced significant turnover in

17. Jamtgaard, "Mission of the Atonement," in Ford, *Twelve Tales Untold*, 70.

18. Spirit of Grace at Mission of the Atonement website.

the thirty years since Mission of the Atonement was formed. Just in the first two years of its existence, the parish dealt with the resignation of the Roman Catholic Archbishop and the transfer of the auxiliary bishop, and soon afterward, the death of the American Lutheran Church bishop who had given his blessing to the endeavor only nine days earlier. But the parish persevered and has built new relationships of oversight and counsel with each successive generation of bishops of both traditions. Admittedly, these relationships have been at times warmer than others, and sometimes have needed to fly under the radar. But the parish's ministry and mission have never been challenged by either judicatory.

Ministry and Membership

The various pastors and priests who have served at Mission of the Atonement consider themselves to be clergy to the entire congregation and not just to those of their own denominational tradition. Evangelical Lutheran Church in America pastor Laurie Larson Caesar has served this parish since 1996. Both Lutheran and Catholic members served on the call committee that hired her. She recounts a favorite moment in ministry when she overheard a seven-year-old Catholic girl say to her mother: "When I grow up, I want to be a priest like Father Laurie." Pastor Laurie says emphatically, "She is in every way a part of my community."[19] When Pastor Laurie arrived, her counterpart was a Roman Catholic priest, Father Matt Tumulty, whose title was priest moderator. Her Catholic partner in ministry now is Kathy Truman, a female Roman Catholic lay leader. Truman has approval from the diocesan chancellor to preach. Catholic representatives from the parish are welcome to participate in the Lutheran synod assembly with voice and vote.

As at Church of the Holy Apostles, ministry to interdenominational marriages and families is a part of the parish's charism. John Buesseler, a twenty-year member, noted, "We have always been a multi-denominational family. Over time what has really kept us here is the community, the people, the authenticity, the honesty, the intellectual challenge, the acceptance that just keep stimulating us to want to stay. It is not being Catholic, Lutheran, or whatever. It is the mix in the stew of all these different faith traditions that I think makes it really rich for us here."[20] Confirmation classes are taught ecumenically, with young people of both traditions in class together. The confirmation rites are separate, tradition-specific, and generally offered biennially.

19. Spirit of Grace at Mission of the Atonement, Caesar, interview.
20. Spirit of Grace at Mission of the Atonement, Buesseler, interview.

How Worship Works

On a Sunday morning in August 2015, about thirty Lutherans and forty Roman Catholics gathered for worship. The worship pattern has been consistent since the early 1990s. The parish alternates annually between use of the ELCA liturgical calendar (odd-numbered years) and the Roman Catholic liturgical calendar (even-numbered years). Worship is Eucharistic on three of the Sundays of every month. On those Sundays, the two communities share the liturgy of the Word. Currently, preaching alternates between the Lutheran pastor and the Catholic lay leader. A retired Roman Catholic clergyman presides at the Roman Catholic Eucharist; the Lutheran pastor celebrates the Lutheran Eucharist. The transition occurs between the service of the Word and the Eucharist: as they share the peace, one of the groups moves to an adjoining worship space with an altar. The Eucharist is then celebrated simultaneously in separate but nearby worship spaces.

In interviews with Michael Nelson in 2006, parishioners described the pain of separation for the Eucharist and the long-standing practice of singing each other to separate space: "Father Matt said when we sing to each other, as the congregation separates, think of the pain of that separation. . . . It has always been very meaningful to me, to think of the pain of that separation."[21] In 2015, the sentiment persisted. That pain is the expression of longing for the day when the Eucharist can be fully shared together at one altar; that longing is also expressed in the palpable love these parishioners make visible to one another as they share the peace, singing, and, in some cases, literally dancing as half of the congregation travels out of the sanctuary.

One of the parish's founding Catholic members explained: "What brought me here was the fact that it was supposed to be ecumenical, and that was something that was deep in my heart. I felt that we were all brothers and sisters regardless of what church denomination we belonged to, and that is what keeps me here. That, and just the hope that someday there will be openness for all congregations, for all churches to worship together. I just cannot see going back to a mainline denomination of whatever church. It just would not feel right."[22]

On the fourth Sunday of the month, the congregation worships using the joint Lutheran-Roman Catholic Service of the Word, which was approved by both denominations in 1986 for shared common prayer. Using this liturgy allows the congregation to stay together for the entire service once a month, and a potluck lunch afterwards provides a shared breaking of bread. This, too,

21. Nelson, "Living into Unity," 95.
22. Spirit of Grace at Mission of the Atonement, Cannard, interview.

is a long-standing practice of the parish, dating to its earliest days. It is an expression of the commitment to joint worship and prayer now, even as they still wait for the day when the Eucharist can be shared.

Challenges Today

An August 7, 2015 *Huffington Post* article proclaimed Portland to be the "least religious city in the United States." According to the article, forty-two percent of the city's population claims no religious affiliation.[23] When asked about this statistic in an interview the next day, a young adult member of Mission of the Atonement said: "I think the fact that we are in this wider community that is largely un-churched is actually an advantage to a community like this because a lot of those people are much more open to different ideas than people who are regularly attending church."[24] She felt that an ecumenical ministry such as Spirit of Grace is potentially more attractive to the un-churched and unaffiliated people of the city than the standard denominational expressions of Christianity. The Catholic lay leader agreed, "We provide a space where people who have an adverse reaction to church feel comfortable here."[25]

Spirit of Grace is proudly open to lesbian, gay, bisexual, transgendered, and queer people. A banner headline on the parish web page proclaims, "LGBTQ Welcome HERE!" The congregation is affiliated with Reconciling in Christ, the name for Lutheran parishes that publicly welcome LGBT persons. The congregation is also a member of the Community of Welcoming Congregations, an Oregon-Washington advocacy group working for full LGBT equality. A parish group marches in the annual Portland Gay Pride Parade. This could be a touchy matter, but the dual denominational affiliation provides a bit more leeway in this regard since the ELCA is officially open and affirming to partnered gays and lesbians.

Interfaith engagement has also been a hallmark of Spirit of Grace since the September 11, 2001 attacks in New York City, Washington, DC, and Pennsylvania. Soon afterward, the parish entered into a covenant relationship for prayer, conversation, and shared learning with nearby Bilal Mosque in Beaverton. This relationship continues today, sixteen years later.

---

23. Blumberg, "30 Least Religious Cities."
24. Spirit of Grace at Mission of the Atonement, Miller, interview.
25. Spirit of Grace at Mission of the Atonement, Truman, interview.

Looking Toward the Future—Building and Growing

The parish's history and its 2009 Long-Range Plan detail an extensive program of renovations and additions to the parish building and grounds focused on the themes of becoming welcoming, continuing prophetic call, and expanding impact. The labyrinth outside was built in 2009; the entrance, gathering space, and preschool were renovated in 2016. Inclusivity, outreach, dialogue, and welcome are hallmarks of this congregation. "I think the word intentionality is really important," a long-term member reflected. "The people who are here have all made a decision; I want to go to that church. We do not have just a bunch of—what I heard growing up—Sunday Catholics. So intentionality. We choose to be here and therefore I think we come with a more open heart."[26]

HOPE AND EXPECTATION

The remarkable churches described in this chapter were formed in expectation that full communion, or even visible unity, between Roman Catholicism, Lutheranism, and Anglicanism was just on the horizon. They are Advent people, still waiting and watching, keeping the faith through the decades. Will this model thrive and even expand? The challenges are significant, but the possibilities are intriguing. Michael Lee Nelson, a United Methodist pastor and ecumenist, developed a proposal for a Roman Catholic-United Methodist Ecumenical Parish in his 2006 Doctor of Ministry thesis. Perhaps a United Methodist conference and its counterpart Roman Catholic diocese will take up the challenge and the call. In the meantime, the Church of the Holy Apostles and Spirit of Grace at the Mission of the Atonement are shining examples of vibrant ministries that are not afraid to cross boundaries boldly. They are communities of hope and expectation.

26. Spirit of Grace at Mission of the Atonement, Buesseler, interview.

4

Multiple Denominational Affiliations

READERS OF A CERTAIN age will remember the television sitcom *Three's Company*. It featured two women and a man who shared an apartment and could not have been more different from one another. In the end, they stuck together opposite a suspicious landlord reluctant to tolerate their living arrangement. The show's popularity could be attributed not only to our human curiosity about other people's unconventional social arrangements, but also the sheer wonder of the duration of three or more people living together in such close quarters. The thought triggers one's own memories (happy or not) of being a roommate in a college dormitory or sharing space with tenants in a house. These are usually thought to be temporary associations brought on by education or work or a transitional life event. But, three or more congregations, together for the long term? What's that about?

In some ways, this is the curiosity of congregations housing multiple denominational affiliations, some or all of which may not be in full communion relationships. Their members have learned deep practices of respect and become, in a sense, denominationally multilingual in a specific context. How do they hold it all together without falling into lowest common denominator practices? Keep in mind that none of the churches discussed in this chapter describe themselves as "inter-denominational." They seek to be true to their communions, but may experience more difficulties than two-traditioned parishes, as, for instance, when one of the three or four traditions has fewer members and resources, or judicatory support is uneven. While those may be problems shared with their two-tradition counterparts, they are magnified where three or more are gathered.

If two traditions in full communion is analogous to marriage, three or more assorted traditions might appear more unconventional, like a commune or a refugee camp of small congregations combining because they have nowhere else to go. Are these conclusions accurate? Whether you saw the television sitcom or not, read on and see what you think.

UNITED CHRISTIAN PARISH, RESTON, VIRGINIA

Located in a planned community, United Christian Parish (UCP) in Reston, Virginia unites four denominations: Presbyterian Church, USA, United Church of Christ, Christian Church (Disciples of Christ), and United Methodist. Ecumenists will recognize them as denominations among the four original members of the Consultation on Church Union, an inspirational force for this congregation and its founder, an ecumenically involved Methodist whose original concept was of four separate congregations in the town's four corners that would cooperate as a "united parish." The year was 1973. While financial constraints necessitated that only three physical plants went up—Methodist, Presbyterian, and UCC-Disciples—these functioned as independent, but interrelated, parishes. Better use of resources dictated that one facility be constructed for use by the four groups, first occupied in 2012.

The only immovable feature of the contemporary worship space is the font at the entrance to the room. It is divided into a pool suitable for immersions and a small basin for affusion. "Every time we enter we are encountering our baptism," explained Joan Bell-Haynes, the church's Disciples lead pastor. Baptismal identity as foundational and unitive among the four traditions—even if celebrated and understood differently—marks United Christian's discourse and self-understanding. "We enter and are sent out through baptism,"[1] she explains. Even the cross, with its moveable parts, can be redesigned or placed in different locations, initially a controversial feature to members.

Denominational identities are noted by banners in the worship space for the four denominations, yet the congregation stresses its ecumenical identity as a both/and. Seating is arranged in semi-circular rows around a pulpit designed to resemble an open book, and a large table for weekly communion celebrated during the 11 a.m. service, per Disciples of Christ practice, while an earlier service features communion once a month, more typical of the other three traditions. Combined summer services default to the Disciples practice.

---

1. United Christian Parish, Bell-Haynes, interview.

An Evening Prayer service on Sundays is completely lay-led and also includes communion. Worship is central in United Christian Parish's life, the uniting activity in a mix of four traditions that could easily become unwieldy.

The service the particular Sunday visited was arranged on a four-fold pattern of gathering, proclamation, meal, and sending, with prayers of confession, the peace, two scripture readings, children's sermon, and this Sunday, the commissioning of youth for a mission trip to West Virginia. Two ordained clergy (the Rev. Bell-Haynes and the Rev. Dr. D. Jay Losher, Presbyterian) preached or led other parts of the liturgy while lay elders presided over the table, customary in Disciples practice.

But the sanctuary itself is not so sacrosanct to this congregation that the furniture cannot be moved for the sake of a social outreach program. For instance, a Stop Hunger Now campaign uses the sanctuary as multipurpose space to assemble food for the hungry. Everything is moved for the effort except the immovable font, a reminder of the baptismal call to service.

The potential for unwieldiness is met by a fourteen-page constitution and a thirty-four-page set of bylaws, attempting to cover the differing policies and procedures for the four denominations. As at Brandermill Church (see chapter 2) two hours south of Reston, the Presbyterian practice of ordained ruling elders is maintained amidst other traditions with different concepts of ordination. It is an ordination not to a "session," but to a common Parish Board comprised of elected officials from the congregation.

Though founded by a Methodist, the United Methodist Church's appointment system has been difficult to square with the call systems of the other three partners in this church's experience. There has not been a United Methodist clergy on staff at United Christian Parish since 2000, and the situation is made more difficult by the presence of a new United Methodist church not far from United Christian Parish. Currently, The Rev. Bell-Haynes serves as the one called and installed pastor for the entire church. The Rev. Losher serves as an interim co-pastor, and there is an interim Director of Christian Education in place (also PCUSA). The goal is to have two co-pastors and a Director of Christian Education in place as a full-time leadership team.

Despite such difficulties, Pastor Bell-Haynes has worked to help the parish reassert its ecumenical identity. "Relating to four denominations can be crazy-making, but it has a richness about it you won't find anywhere else,"[2] she says. Or, as noted seminary professor Fred Craddock once said of UCP: "It's like riding four horses at once!"

---

2. United Christian Parish, Bell-Haynes, interview.

TRINITY ECUMENICAL PARISH, SMITH MOUNTAIN LAKE, VIRGINIA

Part of the lure of the idyllic is the opportunity for newness. In this case, the idyllic is the community of Moneta, on Smith Mountain Lake, Virginia, near Roanoke, and the opportunity for newness and creativity is Trinity Ecumenical Parish (TEP). The lake is a recreational and retirement mecca, the result of a dam built in 1963 that attracted development in earnest by the 1980s, including golf courses, marinas, and luxury homes and condominiums. The current population is about 22,000.

The parish grew out of local residents' weekly Bible study in the mid-1980s. Seeing the opportunity to plant an ecumenical congregation, the members of the Bible study approached the Episcopal, Lutheran, and Presbyterian judicatories and sought their guidance. The judicatories commissioned a steering committee headed by a Presbyterian minister and including some of the Bible study participants. Their mission was to explore the possibility of a church at Smith Mountain Lake, resulting in a three-way mission by 1987, with official establishment in 1991 as Trinity Ecumenical Parish. The coordinating document for the parish was the Covenant Agreement, largely the effort of a retired Episcopal priest who was part of the Bible study group. The Covenant Agreement was approved by the three judicatories and by the new congregation and signed by all parties. The building was constructed on land donated by—parishioners report—a local non-member, an admitted agnostic—and dedicated in 1997. Swelling attendance necessitated building and parking lot expansion soon after.[3]

Laity may choose from four categories of affiliation with the parish: membership in the Episcopal, Lutheran, or Presbyterian congregations, or "non-member parishioners" who attend but do not affiliate with one of the three denominations. The three denominational constituencies, however, are agreed that baptisms and confirmations must be tied to one of them; a candidate cannot be initiated "at large." New members receive a three-session orientation on the nature of TEP and how the three traditions work together.

Trinity Ecumenical Parish expects its pastors to be committed to ecumenism and knowledgeable of all three traditions, especially given that they are expected to participate in all three governing boards (vestry, council, and session), all three judicatory assemblies, preside using the liturgies of all three, and provide pastoral care sensitive to the practices of all three. However, the parish does not use a specific term for the shared ministry itself (e.g. union, federated, joint) in its literature. "We did not want to use 'Federated'

3. Trinity Ecumenical Parish website.

(even though some Presbyterians favored the term) because it sounded too 'governmental.'"[4]

An overarching governing board called the Parish Council consists of twelve members (four from each congregation). This council sets facility policy and budget. The Parish Council elects its own president, vice president, and treasurer. The property is held by a non-profit corporation according to the terms of the Covenant Agreement. A yearly annual meeting of the whole parish ratifies the proposed budget and confirms council membership, though other general meetings (called "forums") may be called throughout the year, as necessary, to address other matters of common interest. Having one budget in common among the three constituencies, according to the website. "The parish has a policy of allocating twenty percent of its budget to benevolence. Ten percent is split three ways among the three judicatories. Five percent is split between the three congregations for denominational programs and other ministries of their choice. Another five percent goes to ministry of service, supporting eight to twelve service organizations in the area."[5] Youth ministry is strong, and a joint program fields mission trips, erasing the stereotype of the church as older adult. Two youth from the congregation have entered the ministry, and one is currently involved in campus ministry. The parish operates a thriving pre-school program serving area families.

The parish boasts sixty small group ministries, populated by all three memberships. A strong increment toward community service gives Trinity a high profile in the community. That may be key to what makes the church attractive to non-members who informally affiliate. "We have people who worship here at 8 a.m. and attend their own church later in the morning," reported one parishioner.[6] Trinity's popularity does not prevent its members from self-criticism, as another member remarked, "We're considered the white-collar church here." Yet another said non-members might sometimes say of them, "Oh, you belong to that church that doesn't know what it wants to be."[7]

But the group interviewed agreed that their self-identity as a parish is not in question for them. They believe that "ecumenical" does not mean blasé disregard for particularities. The term "non-denominational" is assiduously avoided. Rather, they commit to recognizing God's power flowing through the three traditions, whereas non-denominationalism is, to them, invested in no structure or tradition. Trinity Ecumenical Parish maintains its own structure, practices, and vocabulary and is meticulously organized, right down to

4. Trinity Ecumenical Parish, Anonymous, interview.

5. Trinity Ecumenical Parish, Bouknight, interview.

6. Trinity Ecumenical Parish, Anonymous, interview.

7. Trinity Ecumenical Parish, Anonymous, interview.

stipulations about facility use by outside groups. There seems to be awareness that many congregants have come from careers in management and leadership and know how to apply their skills to church life. Tradition and flexibility are down to a science at Smith Mountain Lake.

Conversation also revealed a strong desire to learn and share differences, for instance, in the context of the still-running Smith Mountain Lake Bible study. "Agreements outweigh inconsequential things we don't agree on," said one. "Different perspectives widen our vision of faith," said another.[8] They agree that exposure to different perspectives invites growth, whereas resistance to other views creates fear. A Protestant theological center holds with Pastor Bouknight's observation, "The Word of God brings us together."[9]

The particularities are balanced by the unity, and all that can be shared, members and pastor agree, must. The 8 a.m. Sunday service uses an ecumenical Eucharistic liturgy, followed by shared, long- and short-term Sunday school forums and classes for all ages. The 10:30 a.m. service features a monthly rotation among the three liturgies with communion celebrated on the first Sunday. Rotation for special services such as Christmas Eve and Easter insure that all three rites are represented annually. All are celebrated by the parish's current pastor, a Lutheran. A music director oversees one parish choir, hand bells, and a folk music group that occasionally provides music for services. The worship space reflects the ecumenical, post-Vatican II liturgical consensus, featuring a free-standing altar behind which clergy are seated.

Besides the pastor, and eventually, the new associate pastor, there is a parish nurse on staff who divides her time with the local Catholic church, a preschool director, the music director, lay pastoral assistant, and two administrative assistants. A fourteen-member Stephen Ministry team provides listening ears and care for people in grief or other distress.

PINAWA CHRISTIAN FELLOWSHIP, PINAWA, MANITOBA

The seeds of the Pinawa Christian Fellowship (PCF) lie in a small nuclear research town in northern Ontario, Deep River. The nuclear race of the decades following the Second World War led to the development of a second nuclear research facility, a company town named Pinawa, to be carved out of the forest, rock, and marshes in eastern Manitoba. A group of Deep River residents, who would soon populate Pinawa—scientists, engineers, and technical staff—met in early 1963 to explore the possibility that they would not only work together,

8. Trinity Ecumenical Parish, Anonymous, interview.
9. Trinity Ecumenical Parish, Bouknight, interview.

but worship together, in their new home. The company (Atomic Energy of Canada) noted that the first building that would be ready for community use would be the public school. The "Pinawa Church Group" agreed to create their initial plans around the use of this school, with a purpose-built church building to come later. "Later" has yet to come, and the Pinawa Christian Fellowship still meets, by choice, in the school.

The Pinawa organizing group worked hard through 1963 to inform and convince denominational leaders of their plans. The first PCF worship service took place in November 1963, with the support of six denominations: Anglican, Baptist, Lutheran, Mennonite, Presbyterian, and United Church of Canada. Initially, the six denominations provided Sunday ministry on a weekly rotation. In 1965, they called their first resident ordained minister, from the United Church of Canada. They have been served by ordained personnel from the Anglican, United, and Presbyterian churches since then; their current minister, a Presbyterian, has served the congregation for twenty-one years. The shared ministry has also produced at least four pastors for others— members who have gone on to train and serve in the Anglican, Mennonite, Presbyterian, and United churches.

By the early twenty-first century, the nuclear research facility at Pinawa had been decommissioned, and the town has transitioned into a resort and retirement community. The Lutherans left the shared ministry early, in 1966, to form their own congregation—citing, in part, their desire to provide a Lutheran confirmation program for youth, based on Luther's *Small Catechism*. Pinawa Lutheran Church currently shares summer worship with the PCF. The Baptists, always a numerically small but active portion of the congregation, lost the support of their denominational body in the mid-1990s. Still, a four-denomination shared ministry remains, a "many-faceted jewel" that continues to serve its community and the surrounding region.

COMMUNITY CHURCH AT TELLICO VILLAGE, TENNESSEE

Like Reston and Smith Mountain Lake, Tellico Village, thirty miles south of Knoxville, Tennessee, is a planned community, especially designed with retirees in mind. Founded in 1986, the church has grown along with its appealing natural surroundings. Church membership stands near 1,000 in a community of 5,791 (2010 census). The median age is sixty-seven; the median income is $68,771.[10] The community is laid out around three golf courses along the Tennessee River, popular for fishing and boating. Streets have historic Cherokee names such as Tanasi and Chota, and golf carts are as common as cars. The Community Church is a commodious, steepled structure that says to any passerby that they have reached the center of "The Village." Only a modest strip of restaurants, offices, and a gas station break up the golf courses, waterways, and Tennessee woodlands. A large war memorial next to the church commemorates the service of "Villagers" in World War II, Korea, and Vietnam.

The Rev. Devin Phillips is one of three pastors on staff. The church has had more in the past and would like to return to a higher number to better meet the congregation's needs. Phillips serves as "Pastor of Connections," focused on "connecting guests, members, and volunteers to the church."[11] He and his two colleagues are ordained Baptists, though past clergy have been a mix of other denominations. The congregation styles itself "inter-denominational" and maintains no official ties with any denomination, though it is affiliated with the International Council of Community Churches.

The church's denominational composition is broad—everything from Eastern Orthodox and Roman Catholic through the gamut of the Protestant mainline to conservative evangelical traditions. This reflects a breadth not typical of the surrounding Tennessee religious landscape, among many contrasts "The Village" has with its environment.

"It's a beautiful thing," Phillips says of his church's diversity. "People who have been spurned by fights in other churches find a home here. Believers in infant baptism sit alongside those baptized as believers with little debate," he says.[12] The currently Baptist pastoral staff have no problem pastoring among a diversity of beliefs and practices. The church's mission statement is Christocentric and non-specific about controversial practices.

Communion is observed weekly at the 8 a.m. Sunday service, to the satisfaction of members from sacramental backgrounds. The 10:15 a.m. service includes Eucharist on the first Sunday of the month, familiar to less liturgical Protestants. Wednesday evenings feature topical studies that change periodically, with communion on the first Wednesday that offers wine along with the customary grape juice. The table, like all this congregation's activities, is open to all. Communion liturgies vary by month, drawing on resources of different traditions.

10 US Census Bureau Fact Finder.

11. Community Church at Tellico Village website.

12. Community Church at Tellico Village, Philips, interview.

What might appear to be challenging demographics, given the community's retirement age, belies the fact of this church's growth. Youth and young families have ebbed and flowed through the years, but longevity plus perhaps access to recreation, lots of activities, and mild winters have conspired to create optimal circumstances for the people of Tellico Village. But with age, explained Phillips, comes a unique set of pastoral needs. "How do I make my life matter?" ask seniors. The topic is addressed at Wednesday evening studies, where the staff make a concerted effort to meet twin objectives—answer their members' existential questions and improve their biblical literacy. Phillips notes unevenness in parishioners' biblical knowledge, sometimes a factor in their early life experiences or their native denomination's standards. Phillips cites biblical interpretation as most likely to mark differences among members, which range from inerrancy to symbolic readings—these questions commonly generate discussion at Bible study more than difference in practices surrounding baptism or communion. The congregation has no definitive statement on scriptural authority. "It's a fine tango that has to be done with grace and love" he said.[13]

Where members do not disagree is in service. They are united in outreach, having generated several community service organizations and continuous participation in Habitat for Humanity building projects. The congregation's affluence has been put to good use in the community. Such service has been instrumental in attracting Tellico Villagers who, in retirement, make a return to the church from having been skeptical of it because of its burdensome divisiveness. Phillips suggests a similarity between the familiar reports of millennials becoming "nones," and their senior counterparts becoming "dones," having left the church. Seeing the good being done through the church has inspired recommitment on the part of some Villagers who may have expected only sunny days of golf and boating, not community outreach.

Besides service, Phillips says what is good about Tellico Village Community Church is a counter to what he hears in popular discourse about Christianity as a divisive, abusive force. "I wish more people could see this," he muses. "I wish this unity were more present in our world."[14]

---

13. Community Church at Tellico Village, Philips, interview.
14. Community Church at Tellico Village, Philips, interview.

UNITY IN A HARD-WORKING TOWN: FIRST FEDERATED CHURCH, NORTH JACKSON, OHIO

North Jackson, Ohio is situated between Akron and Youngstown, and thus in the buckle of the Rust Belt. Industry once flourished here, amid broad, flat farmland and prospering communities. What is left in the early twenty-first century is the remnant of a former industrial glory. Service sector jobs predominate. The federation of three congregations in North Jackson—German Reformed (pre-United Church of Christ), Presbyterian, and Disciples, occurred in 1928, and involved sacrifice. The Reformed gave up a little liturgy, such as a General Confession, the Disciples gave up the most, conceding to infant baptism as the norm for the congregation, and the Presbyterians initially asserted (providing as they did the meeting space), "our building, our rules!" Local Lutherans and Methodists were invited to join in the federation, but declined. First Federated "started out of a place of want," explains the current pastor, The Rev. Jack Acri. "That attitude has followed generation upon generation. In 1932 the women's guild sent $9.00 to Chinese missions out of their total $1500.00 in treasury for that year!"[15]

Other features of this congregation's life, however, suggest abundance and generosity. Behind the chancel is an immense storage room full of canned goods for the needy in a community prone to poverty. An active youth group recently went on a mission trip to West Virginia. "They get service," said Pastor Acri. "This church is meaningful to people who have come from narrower church experiences. The openness, expansiveness, and generosity of spirit is what they appreciate most."[16] This oasis of temporal and theological generosity is in a context where harsher forms of Christianity take root, as sociologists of religion point out.

Over a lush buffet in the fellowship hall, congregants explained how appreciative they are of the church's ecumenism, openness to change, and how others in the community perceive them. Indifference to denominational allegiance, they all agree, is a point of pride for them. They do not care "who is what." North Jacksonians think of First Federated as "the church that accepts everybody," says one member. "We are a safe place, free of judgment, not just in terms of denomination, but dress, economic standing, and attitude. You're not judged here."[17] While some outsiders identify this openness by saying, according to another member: "Oh, that's the gay church (meaning we welcome

---

15. First Federated Church, Acri, interview.

16. First Federated Church, Acri, interview.

17. First Federated Church, Lawrence, interview.

everyone)"[18] others appreciate the congregation's leadership in addressing issues of poverty and hunger in the community through the pantry. Crowds show up not only for Thanksgiving and Christmas giveaways but bi-weekly distributions. A pre-school program also serves the needs of working families. A thousand dollars is annually donated for school supplies. First Federated is filling a niche for characteristically broad-minded, service-oriented mainline Protestantism in this community.

Sunday worship features both emergent/contemporary and traditional styles. Congregants say the early, contemporary service appeals to youth and young families while the later service is described as "calm, and "deeper." Both answer felt needs of members for either a high energy level or spiritual depth. While there are youth, but no adult Sunday School classes between the two services, Pastor Acri teaches a confirmation class geared toward a hands-on learning experience for confirmands. He explains that he encourages pupils to explore the questions they ask rather than accept simple answers from him or anyone else. "I want them to grasp a sense of theological complexity,"[19] he says. Confirmands accept one of the three denominations toward the end of the course, being directed to research UCC, Disciples, and PCUSA websites and report back their findings as to the nature and ethos of the three.

The church had a practice of alternating pastors among the three denominations, though no Presbyterian has served in twenty years. When asked about relationships with their three judicatories, members laugh and say, "we relate to them as little as possible." Though there were at one time three different governing boards in the church, today there is only one, though mission support and benevolence dollars are sent equally to the three denominations.

"People who come our way don't want to hear a party line. They want the freedom to explore and question, but in a family-like atmosphere,"[20] said one parishioner. And so it goes in North Jackson, where this three-way, federated parish is making a difference in its own quiet way. The fact of the three denominations symbolizes the inclusivity and generosity toward which they strive in all things.

SO, IS THREE COMPANY?

Or four? The saying suggests inconvenience, complication, or "cat herding." The five churches featured here agree that it is complicated, with uneven

18. First Federated Church, McKinney, interview.

19. First Federated Church, Acri, interview.

20. First Federated Church, Andrews, interview.

levels of support from judicatories, and one or more traditions outnumbered. And yet, these examples of three and four-way unity have persisted, even flourished, making distinctive ecumenical witness in their respective communities. Although the North Jackson folk can border on sounding almost non-denominational in their self-description, they do not qualify as a non-denominational church. They have been richly formed by three traditions, however unevenly at times, by rotating pastors and preserving practices from all three. A theological foundation in baptism gives United Christian Parish in Reston a liturgical grounding and point of departure from which four diverse communions can share their gifts with one another. Of these, perhaps it is Trinity Ecumenical Parish in Smith Mountain Lake that most sharply maintains lines of distinction within a remarkable unity in a carefully engineered, local ecumenical structure.

Ultimately, the real unifying thread is the Spirit. An infectious enthusiasm about their lives together typifies these congregations. There is a strong desire to be present to one another and to offer themselves as a challenge to their communities. It may well be that being in planned communities such as Reston and Smith Mountain Lake, or, in Pinawa, a community typified by a common objective, offers permission to be different. These congregations embrace their experimental status as the work of the Spirit for the sake of a more imaginative, daring way of being church for the world.

5

The Long Generation

"WE'RE JUST STUBBORN!"[1] THAT is how the people of Huff's Union Church describe themselves. Their Lutheran and Reformed ancestors in the rolling hills of Berks County, Pennsylvania since 1744 would have proudly agreed. Sturdy German settlers found their way there through Penn's Forest to farm and pass along a heritage to successive generations. Their endurance, they would argue, was not always a foregone conclusion, especially if it had been left to outside forces. And it is a grasp of such forces, and the reasons why they prevailed, that are key to understanding their history. But first, a quick tour of the longer story is necessary to understand the roots of a church like Huff's.

"Union" churches are among the oldest ecumenical congregations in North America, with roots in the sixteenth-century European Reformation. The largest concentration is found in southeastern Pennsylvania, the home of a still-evident German ethos that brought Lutheran and Reformed Christians together in the sharing of facilities. Church buildings both united and divided them. In the eighteenth-century beginnings, both congregations shared a structure but with separate clergy, worship services, and catechesis. This was how Union congregants worked cooperatively, whether it was German ethnicity in a sea of English or scarce resources that kept them together. These were the reasons and the arrangements at Huff's, as at other Union congregations in the area, until recently.

Many of these churches did not survive their denominational marriages; housekeeping became unbearable, and they separated. Or, at times, regional judicatories forced separation. Such a story is told in many places in eastern

---

1. Huff's Union Church, Arner, interview.

Pennsylvania, where a United Church of Christ and a Lutheran Church sit across the road from one another. But for other congregations such as Huff's, separation was seldom entertained. Their determination to make union work matched everything else about who they were and how they understood themselves as a congregation. The story of the Union Church requires a brief glance at the sixteenth-century roots and the cultural dynamics at work among the Pennsylvania Dutch in the colonial and Early Republic periods.

A GOLDEN HISTORY: SIXTEENTH-CENTURY BEGINNINGS THROUGH THE EARLY AMERICAN REPUBLIC

Lutherans and Reformed were divided by a common vision of the need for church renewal. These differences, which may have looked (at best) like nuances to outsiders, were matters of truth and falsity for many of the quarreling children of the Reformers Martin Luther and John Calvin. The shared theological consensus in the Reformation's doctrine of justification by grace through faith apart from works of the law was frayed around the edges by differing views of the Lord's Supper, predestination, worship styles, polity, and other matters.

Between Luther and Calvin stood Luther's associate, Philip Melanchthon (1497–1560), whose efforts at harmonization among discordant theologies are enshrined in his writings. While he was author of the 1530 version of the *Augsburg Confession*, a succinct explanation of Lutheran teaching on key contested points in the debate with the Catholic Church, Melanchthon offered a revised version a decade later, called the *Variata*, in efforts to soften differences on another front, namely, between Lutheran and Reformed parties. Such a mediating position held sway until differences solidified in the 1560s, when Lutherans and Reformed were hardened into two separate families of churches, each with its own intramural nuances and quarrels.

The Palatinate region of southwest Germany saw the rise of the German Reformed Church under its Elector, Frederick III (1515–76). This church's position was summed up in the 1563 *Heidelberg Catechism* penned by Zacharias Ursinus and Caspar Olevianus, and the 1561 *Second Helvetic Confession*, authored by Huldrich Zwingli's successor Heinrich Bullinger. These documents formed the foundation of a separate church with a character distinct from that of Lutheranism, especially when many purists in the latter camp came to see the *Variata* as a watered-down betrayal of Luther's sharply defined doctrines.

However, Lutherans, among themselves, were theologically variegated. Differences on free will, the uses of the law, and predestination, were taken up in yet another document, the 1577 *Formula of Concord*, which, along with Luther's catechisms, *Augsburg Confession*, and other documents, was assembled into the *Book of Concord* in 1580, the complete volume of Lutheran authoritative teachings or "symbols." Reformed Churches, too, featured varying levels of commitment to intramural debates, particularly around predestination.

As they matured, German Reformed and Lutherans placed a common value on confessional statements, an educated clergy, and a focus on clear, biblical preaching and catechesis. An orthodox movement in both stressed correct teaching and reinforced their differing formulations on the Lord's Supper and teachings on election, even if, taken as a whole, the constellation of teaching documents and practices from the two churches form an extended theological family in which shared traits and family resemblances strike the observer's eye.

If theology divided them, temporal circumstances and a reaction in their ranks against rigid orthodoxy united them. They lived together, intermarried, and suffered a common lot in the economically and politically uncertain world of the late sixteenth through eighteenth centuries. These temporal hardships would precipitate first small, then progressively larger, waves of immigration to the American middle colonies starting in 1683.[2] Following a new generation of leaders in both traditions who stressed personal experience over doctrine, members of Reformed and Lutheran churches, especially in the Palatinate, sang hymns that stirred their hearts to individual testimony of conversion and holiness in addition to—or more crucial than—confessional subscription. This common pietism became a dynamo bridging the confessional gaps and was carried by the faithful of both stripes as they made their way across the Atlantic. Their common language, culture, piety, and Reformation experience proved stronger than the theological debates between them. External forces in their new home, would push them even closer together when they stepped off the boats. Conflict and cohesion continued in the New World, even within the walls of their shared churches.

The first recorded Union Churches were established in Catskill and Dutchess counties, New York, by Reformed pastor John Frederick Hager and his Lutheran counterpart, Joshua von Kocherthal, who had shepherded immigrants from the Palatinate via Holland and England in 1709–10. Discouraging prospects in New York drove the settlers to Pennsylvania, where they were joined by increasing numbers of their compatriots in the early 1700s. Numbers of Union congregations grew from twelve in 1748 to seventy-eight in

2. Glatfelter, *Pastors and People*, 3.

1776, to 100 in 1800—almost half the total number of Lutheran and Reformed churches in Pennsylvania—though most were concentrated in several counties in the southeastern corner of the state.[3]

REASONS FOR THE UNION CHURCH PHENOMENON

The commonly shared Pietist phenomenon continued in earnest in eighteenth-century Pennsylvania, where Germans of Dunker, Mennonite, Moravian, Quaker, Schwenkfelder, Lutheran, and Reformed identities often met together. Arguably, this broadly common stress on personal experience and heartfelt faith was a stronger bonding force than the common language, as the visiting English evangelist George Whitefield was warmly received in Philadelphia by the Germans there of all stripes in 1740.[4] One Reformed pastor quipped: "I am Reformed; I am also a Lutheran; I am also a Mennonite. A Christian is everything."[5]

Fissures in this ecumenism of the heart appeared where differences were noticeable between the Moravian, Anabaptist (Mennonite, Dunker), Quaker, and Schwenkfelder "sectarians" on the one hand, and Reformed and Lutheran "church people" on the other. Members of both groups disparaged one another as, respectively, uneducated or unconverted. A moderate reassertion of their traditions came with the leadership of the Swiss Reformed Michael Schlatter and the German Lutheran Henry M. Muhlenberg. As the latter notably said, "The church must be planted." These two leaders struggled to secure fellow clergy from Europe to serve in Penn's Forest even as they maintained cordial relations with one another, still united by a common pietism and often ministering among one another's flocks.[6] A synthesis of Pietist and institutional currents made the concept of the local Union Church a sensible, restrained form of ecumenism that serviced other needs as well, whether practical matters such as clergy shortage, financial limitations, and common language, or the more complex issue of the unique Pennsylvania Dutch form of cultural assimilation in the American colonies, to all of which we now turn.

Another reason for cooperation among the "church people" was that clergy were scarce in eighteenth-century colonial America, so the services of a

3. Glatfelter, *Pastors and People*, 3. See also Macauley, "Social and Intellectual History," 316–22.

4. Longenecker, *Piety and Tolerance*, 71.

5. Attributed to Henry Antes by Henry Boehm, "Second Faithful Warning and Admonition," May 19, 1743, *Life and Letters of Boehm*, 378, cited in Longenecker, *Piety and Tolerance*, 77.

6. Longenecker, *Piety and Tolerance*, 95.

German-speaking minister of either stripe was appreciated by Reformed and Lutherans, especially when a baby awaited baptism or some other pastoral act was needed. Some early pastors noted in their journals when they had performed such acts for the opposite denomination, though often the difference was not mentioned at all. Months stretched between clergy visits to a typical settlement. Language proved a barrier as well, keeping German-speakers in enclaves less integrated into the English-speaking majority. Church building was a daunting task for people with limited finances, making the idea of a common building an attractive solution. Thus, the *gemeinschaftliche Kirche*—Union Church—was born.[7]

Pastors typically served several of these union congregations at once, rotating duties so as to be present on alternate Sundays at one Union Church. For instance, Reformed might hold services when their minister was present on first and third Sundays, the Lutherans taking second and fourth. The congregations maintained their common facility (through a joint treasury for the purpose), burial ground, and sometimes commonly held communion ware. A joint board of trustees with equal representation from both churches cared for property issues. Otherwise, church business germane to the Reformed was conducted by the Consistory, while Lutherans maintained a local Church Council.

There is little evidence that laity sensed that their denominational identities were compromised through this arrangement. Respective ministers catechized and confirmed their pupils separately. Communion was rarely ever shared together, since it was rarely celebrated at this time by either denomination in the colonies (twice a year for Reformed and, ideally, three times among Lutherans, at Christmas, Easter, and Pentecost). Architecturally, some Union Churches had two entrances, one for each denomination. Some clergy worried that too much unionism was not good for the soul, as when the Lutheran patriarch Muhlenberg counseled "the way of love" over "the way of equity," by which he meant that Christian charity did not require the financial, or worse, theological, entanglements made possible by the Union Church.[8]

UNION CHURCHES IN CULTURAL PERSPECTIVE

What factors, then, in the culture shared by Lutheran and Reformed immigrants to Pennsylvania (the so-called "Pennsylvania Dutch") grounded the proliferation of Union Churches in the colonial and Early Republic periods?

7. Glatfelter, *Pastors and People*, 162–63.
8. Glatfelter, *Pastors and People*, 169.

For one, both churches were faced with maintaining their traditions, which always meant determining the appropriate degree of assimilation to an American culture shaped largely by British sensibilities. The Pennsylvania Dutch struck this balance with an intricate dance between their own German identity and the possibilities the new society afforded them. There were foundational differences, however, between Anglo-American and German cultures that made cohesion with the wider culture less likely for the Germans.

That is, the German identity shared by Lutherans and Reformed in Pennsylvania was more than a matter of language and custom but also meant political philosophy and convictions about the nature and purpose of the church derived from the Reformation. Where the British colonists had definite notions of liberty rooted in an individualism stemming from Lockean philosophical assumptions, the Pennsylvania Dutch conceived their freedom in terms brought with them from the Rhineland, where Reformed and Lutheran pietism habituated them in a "personal freedom [ensconced within] the authority of local custom and church structure to provide order as an effective means of social control," what Steven Nolt calls "peasant republicanism."[9]

This traditionalism saw advantage in the new republic's democratic freedom, that is, German immigrants valued freedom from outside meddling. The wider social and political cultures that were evolving created space as much for ethnic separatism as they did for ethnic cohesion. Pennsylvania Germans chose the former, minimizing entanglement with Anglo-American culture, language, and values. A strong commitment to localism and their freedom from suspicion of larger bodies exercising distant control over local affairs marked eighteenth and nineteenth century Pennsylvania Dutch life as a whole before it marked the specifically Amish branch of that culture with which many readers might readily identify it. Religion was an ethnic marker and means of differentiation from the wider culture.

These shared "peasant republican" ideals made Lutheran-Reformed rapprochement seem natural. Church life was a local affair of self-governance. Congregations called and dismissed their own pastors—if they even had one—and passed on the ethos of the two traditions through catechesis, liturgy, and ethnic identity, and forms of pastoral care. It was this strong sense of freedom from outside entanglements and localism that was shared by the two churches, even to the point that Lutheran efforts to bring together various synods in other states into a General Synod in 1820 were rebuffed by Pennsylvania Lutherans in favor of union with their Reformed neighbors. Joint efforts were already underway by 1787 with the joint administration of Franklin College in Lancaster, Pennsylvania, support for one another's publications, and

9. Nolt, *Foreigners in Their Own Land*, 30–31.

the sending of delegates to one another's synod meetings. Support for this regional ecumenism was strong enough to stop efforts to unite the Pennsylvania Ministerium with Samuel Simon Schmucker's General Synod and re-direct efforts toward unity with the state's Reformed churches. The common denominator was not theological precision (though, arguably, neither was that the object for the General Synod) but common ethnicity, a trait Pennsylvania Lutherans sensed they had with the Reformed more than with Lutherans in other states.[10]

Pastor Johann A. Probst's *The Reunion of the Lutheran and Reformed* (1826) expressed the sentiments of many pastors and leaders of his generation. While Schmucker could argue for intra-Lutheran unity based on a lightly-held set of confessional affirmations, opponents of such unity in Pennsylvania argued similarly for union with the Reformed and against Schmucker's platform. The differences between the two churches belonged to the past; now was the time, and America was the place, to forge unity based on common love of ethnicity and local control, which outweighed the debates of the past.[11]

This early nineteenth-century development at the regional level naturally sprang from the success of local Lutheran-Reformed Union Churches. Union congregations in this scheme were a step along the way toward what Probst envisioned as the alleviation of needless duplication of parishes and pastors among the two groups. An unofficial hymnal, *das Gemeinschaftliche Gesangbuch*, had been published in 1817 as part of the Reformation anniversary commemoration and was widely used among Union Churches.[12] Opposition to tying Pennsylvania Lutheran identity to "Dutch" ethnicity became stronger, however, by 1842, when some pastors balked at their experience of an ethnic hothouse closed to the winds blowing through the nation in the Second Great Awakening with its voluntarism and social reform. However, later assertions of Lutheran and Reformed doctrinal particularity as part of new generation of clergy and synod leaders supported efforts to split Union Churches, though the earlier sentiments toward grassroots ecumenism, even if ethnically motivated, remained strong.[13]

If by the late eighteenth and early nineteenth century, laity in Union Churches were generally content and their clergy cautious, outsiders admired the curiosity of union churches when they visited Pennsylvania. John Adams wrote to wife Abigail on January 24, 1777: "There is an elegant Stone Church

10. Nolt, *Foreigners in Their Own Land*, 120ff.

11. Nolt, *Foreigners in Their Own Land*, 121; cf. Nelson, *Lutherans in North America*, 122ff.

12. Nolt, *Foreigners in Their Own Land*, 113.

13. Nolt, *Foreigners in Their Own Land*, 125.

here built by the Dutch People, by whom the Town is chiefly inhabited, and what is remarkable because uncommon, the Lutherans and Calvinists united to build this Church, and the Lutheran and Calvinist Minister[s] alternately officiate in it."[14] And Philadelphia physician Benjamin Rush glowingly commented:

> The Lutherans compose a great proportion of the German citizens of the state [of Pennsylvania]. Many of their churches are large and splendid. The German Presbyterians are the next to them in numbers. Their churches are likewise large and furnished, in many places, with organs. The clergy, belonging to these churches, have moderate salaries, but they are punctually and justly paid. In the country they have glebes which are stocked and occasionally worked by their congregations. The extra expenses of their ministers, in all their excursions to their ecclesiastical meetings, are borne by their respective congregations. By this means the discipline and general interests of their churches are preserved and promoted. The German Lutherans and Presbyterians live in great harmony with each other, insomuch that they often preach in each other's churches, and in some instances unite in building a church, in which they both worship at different times. This harmony between two sects, one [sic] so much opposed to each other, is owing to the relaxation of the Presbyterians in some of the peculiar doctrines of Calvinism. I have called them Presbyterians, because most of them object to being designated by the name of Calvinists.[15]

The approving observations of these observers came in tandem with admiration for German thrift and exacting work ethic.

Sunday schools began to appear and quickly gain popularity in North American churches by the late eighteenth century. They presented a unique opportunity and challenge for Union Churches—worrisome for clergy, but empowering for laity. Sunday schools became a kind of "third congregation" run jointly by laity of both traditions. The church school was a haven for lay leadership, having its own officers and treasuries apart from either congregation. The influence these officers could leverage troubled pastors unfavorable toward lay leadership and a competing force that amalgamated two traditions

---

14. L. H. Butterfield, ed., *Adams Family Correspondence* (Cambridge: Harvard University Press, 1963) 2:148, cited in Glatfelter, *Pastors and People*, 170.

15. Rush, *Account of the Manners*, 94–96.

when the worship schedule and separate polities suggested the boundaries proper to the union relationship.[16]

THE COMMISSION ON THE WELFARE OF THE UNION CHURCH

Recognizing that the Union Church was subject to an array of unique problems, thirty-two representatives from Evangelical and Reformed and Lutheran judicatories in Pennsylvania and Maryland gathered in Reading, Pennsylvania, on November 23, 1948 to formulate the following "Statement on the Union Church":

> Cordial and cooperative fellowship between Lutheran and Evangelical and Reformed Congregations, sharing the same building for Christian service, is a splendid testimony to the Christian ideal, "that they all may be one." It may be necessary for the "union" relationship to continue through coming years for economic or other reasons. There is nothing, however, in the nature of this relationship that should prevent each congregation from participating in the total program of its denomination and supporting the work of the Kingdom through the regular channels of its own denomination.
>
> We, therefore, submit to the "union churches" of our respective denominations the following recommendations:
>
> 1. That each congregation be incorporated separately, and have its own corporate administrative body—Church Council or Consistory.
>
> 2. That the administrative bodies of congregations meet jointly at stated times to make necessary provisions for the use, maintenance and improvement of the property jointly held; and that the expenses incurred in the use, maintenance and improvement of the common property be shared equally by the congregations.
>
> 3. That each congregation have its own separate treasuries and treasurers.
>
> 4. That each congregation make proper and necessary provisions for the gathering and disbursements of its own funds in such a manner as may be authorized and approved by its

---

16. Horace S. Sills, "The Union Church: A Case of Lutheran and Reformed Cooperation" in Zikmund, *Hidden Histories*, 20.

denomination; and that a "duplex envelope" and the "Every-Member-Visitation" or "Kingdom Roll Call" be considered as the most satisfactory means of meeting both the local and benevolent budgets.

5. That, in Union Sunday Schools, the Literature of one of our denominations be used.

6. That each congregation recognize and develop the authorized auxiliary organizations of its own denominations for men, women, and young people, in order that the denominational program may be adequately promoted.[17]

The Commission on the Welfare of the Union Church was born, comprised of representatives from both denominations, first from the eastern Pennsylvania judicatories, with those from central Pennsylvania following in 1950. The commission was charged with the examination of practices and procedures in the Union Churches as a consultative body at the disposal of Union Churches. The commission could upon request conduct a study of a union congregation to determine the best practices for its flourishing. It could also advocate for union congregations seeing no alternative but to split, though only after offering creative solutions to the local obstacles.

The commission used these mandates in their efforts to be responsive to union church needs throughout its brief history, notably its consultative role as articulated in 1951 and 1957 reports, which gave attention to such matters as worship scheduling and building construction. As important as its mandates were the friendships made on the commission, and the connectivity among the churches provided by the commission's visiting consultants.[18]

The commission is long gone, and today, ELCA-UCC Union Churches number thirty-seven, still mostly in eastern Pennsylvania.[19] At their peak, there were some 500 Union Churches, found not only in the Southeastern Pennsylvania epicenter, but in other Lutheran-Reformed strongholds in New York, Ohio, West Virginia, Maryland, Virginia, and North Carolina.[20] According to a report by the United Church of Christ on Multiply-Affiliated Congregations, many Union Churches have become dual congregations, dis-

17. *History of the Commission on the Welfare of the Union Church.*

18. Horace S. Sills, "The Union Church: A Case of Lutheran and Reformed Cooperation" in Zikmund, *Hidden Histories*, 21.

19. Center for Analytics, Research, and Data, United Church of Christ. An additional four UCC-ELCA congregations use designations other than Union to describe their relationship.

20. Horace S. Sills, "The Union Church: A Case of Lutheran and Reformed Cooperation" in Zikmund, *Hidden Histories*, 20.

tinguished by having one membership roll, committee structure, and budget. Others are now better described as federated congregations, meaning they maintain two membership rolls but may have separate governance structures. Federated or dual might now better describe some historic Union Churches whose structures match one or the other description, but the term remains in use as a marker of these congregations' particular heritage.[21] In many instances, the union relationship has endured for generations, as with the still-vibrant example to which we now turn.

HUFF'S UNION CHURCH, ALBURTIS, PENNSYLVANIA

With little early recorded history to confirm, Huff's Union Church was likely founded in 1760, bringing together Reformed (already organized in 1744) with Lutherans and Mennonites in Hereford Township, Pennsylvania. Mennonites have played a lesser role in the union, but, by joint agreement, are welcome to use the structure for services and the cemeteries for burial, so long as the minister is a regularly called and not a "vagabond or visionary" Mennonite.[22] As was often the case, the schoolhouse doubled as a church and a succession of local teachers preached on Sundays. The first joint structure was erected in 1814, followed by the present church, the third structure on the site, built in 1881. The "Laying of the Cornerstone" is a significant anniversary at Huff's and other Union Church buildings as a way to mark the shared ministry enshrined in the building, while the two congregations would continue to commemorate their own separate founding anniversaries. The church's architecture is typical for the region: a two-storey building with a fellowship hall and Sunday school rooms on the ground floor, and a sanctuary on the second floor. The church is flanked by large cemeteries and acres of farmland dotted with gabled rock barns and houses.[23]

Today, Union Churches like Huff's that have been successful for over two centuries may be moving either toward (in UCC parlance) federation or dual arrangements, where one pastor of either tradition is called, all activities are blended, and features of both liturgical traditions are retained. That this blending would evolve was not always a foregone conclusion. As recently as the 1980s, a move was afoot in some UCC and Lutheran judicatories to separate Union Churches into purely single denomination parishes in the name of

21. Billings, *Multiply-Affiliated Congregations*, 5. According to the report, Dual congregations account for 66.5% of the 455 multiple-affiliated UCC congregations; Federated, 27.5%; Union, 5.5%; and 0.5% unknown.

22. Kropa, correspondence, September 22, 2015.

23. For an account of the church history, see the Huff's Union Church website.

doing better evangelism. "Save the Union" buttons were made by some laity, while judicatory leaders feared that "union" was a confusing term that would puzzle prospective members out of darkening church doors. People knew what "Lutheran" was, but "Union"? What's that?

At Huff's "Union" means everything. The evolution of its meaning, though, has been long. From 1760 until the 1980s, the original pattern of two pastors, two traditions, two services, and one building continued. Services were held in each tradition on different Sundays, and each pastor served a charge including two other congregations. By 1990 there was a strong interest in doing more together; clergy started sharing duties and celebrating both liturgies in the church on Sundays, UCC at one service, Lutheran at the other. The pattern would be reversed by years: one year, 8 a.m. was UCC, and 10:15 a.m. was Lutheran, then vice versa. To the laughter of reminiscing parishioners, this agreed-upon pattern was nonetheless voted upon each year. At times the UCC or Lutheran folk would alternate using the smaller chapel across the road from the larger church, while other activities were held in common. All of this was but the prelude to a deepening communion that came in 2000, with the first sole pastor of the congregation, an interim who had been the called UCC pastor. Then, when the Lutheran pastor moved to serve a different congregation, he became the interim for both Lutheran and UCC congregations. Huff's current sole pastor, The Rev. Jane Moffat Kropa, grew up Lutheran but was educated at Lutheran and UCC seminaries. Her fluency in both traditions makes her an ideal leader for a Union Church.

Lutheran and UCC hymnals are tucked in the pew racks and used together in blended liturgies that follow a pattern familiar to both traditions: greeting, confession and forgiveness, Word and sermon and affirmation of faith, offering, prayers, and dismissal. Eucharistic practice presents a potential obstacle easily navigated at Huff's, where "pew communion" (Reformed) and "altar communion" (Lutheran) and "continuous communion" (with communicants lining up for the elements distributed in the front of the church) are used at different services. Efforts are made to keep distribution methodology from becoming less a marker of denominational identity and more a feature of variety enriching for any believer. Nobody in the church stays away because the practice is not "theirs." Both are "theirs." The consensus is, "This is how we do it at Huff's."[24] Theologically, the 1997 *Formula of Agreement* between Reformed and Lutheran denominations paved the way for greater mutual understanding and consensus around matters that have divided the churches. The *Formula* has been a foundational document in the ministry of many Union Church pastors, including Pastor Jane Kropa.

24. Huff's Union Church, group, interview.

The Sunday this author visited was not a communion Sunday, but was otherwise indicative of a typical Sunday at Huff's. There were two services, 8 and 10:30, with Sunday School in between. Pew racks housed the United Church of Christ's, *Evangelical and Reformed Hymnal*, the *Lutheran Book of Worship* and Bibles. Seating is ample, and walking into the sanctuary draws the eye upward to the balconies on three sides, and the large mural of the Ascension over the altar in the apse. An 1817 George Krauss pipe organ stands majestically in the back balcony, where it was repositioned in 1883 during the construction of the present church. In addition to pulpit and lectern, the chancel features a free-standing altar. The formal but relatively simple services followed a liturgical order reflective of both heritages. A bell choir played and youth participated as liturgists at the second service. A third, contemporary service called "Manna" is held by the laity once a month in the small chapel across the road from the main building.

Youth activities and confirmation are important features of Huff's congregational life as a strong, shared, lay-led Sunday School has long been in place here. As in many Union Churches, the pattern was found in a neighboring community in Berks County, where jointly held Sunday Schools met for decades, and children were members of a class before ever being members of a specific church. One member opines that the foundation of harmony at Huff's is the Sunday School itself, a cooperative effort almost since the church's inception.[25]

A united Christian education program made it easy to think in terms of other things being done together, until even worship and pastoral leadership became common. Pastor Kropa explained that confirmation is taught in such a way that both traditions are examined and honored, and candidates are confirmed as members of both denominations. The Heidelberg Catechism and Luther's Small Catechism are taught, along with the theologies of Luther, Zwingli, and Calvin. Eucharistic theology was a major point of contention among the Reformers. A power-point presentation used in Union Church confirmation classes illustrates a harmonizing strategy using three illustrations: the Lutheran "on, with, in, and under"; the Reformed "mystical ascent to heaven"; and the communal table at which Jesus is host. These doctrines represent, according to the curriculum, Christ present in the finite means, Christ transcending finitude, and Christ at the table. Three modes of presence are all affirmed and allowed to stand. Confirmands can spend a lifetime of communing with all three images of what is transpiring in the eucharistic mystery playing at once in their hearts and minds. Such an understanding sees all theological statements as powerful testaments and signposts to spiritual

25. Huff's Union Church, group, interview.

realities that cannot be contained in any one formula. This is what happens when the riches of enduring theological traditions and the existential realities of a stubborn determination to worship together rather than across the road from one another keep together a congregation such as Huff's.

In the past, it was common for interchurch families in Union Churches to confirm children in one or the other denomination according to gender. So if a Lutheran father and Reformed mother were to have boys and girls, the boys would be confirmed Lutheran and the girls, Reformed. Though youth at Huff's Church may align themselves with their ancestral denomination, they generally find it difficult to picture themselves wholly one or the other, since their catechetical formation has profoundly habituated them in the full range of theological reflection both traditions afford. Confirmation instruction remains a centerpiece of congregational life at Huff's, with a great annual confirmation day celebration, usually Pentecost Sunday.

Conflict in this congregation has been minimal and rarely on account of theological differences. Though there have occasionally been members who have left for denominationally purer pastures, current parishioners see conflict coming from the outside. The judicatories to which the church relates have, at one time or another, engaged in "union busting," trying to split up Union Churches in the name of providing a singular identity believed to be less confusing to potential members. Huff's consistently refused to divide. While judicatories may fail to value the union enterprise, Huff's is happy to see itself a "poster child of union churches," in the spirit of their proud stubbornness.

Along these lines, Pastor Kropa told an anecdotal story passed down among area pastors, that the church once had a liturgical parament that was monogrammed "HUC." On seeing it, a visiting cleric balked, saying that sacred monograms such as "IHS" or the Chi Rho were appropriate, but not the congregation's initials, hardly sacred as he believed they were. The congregants defended the parament, believing their unity was worthy of a sacred monogram! Whether the story is true or apocryphal, it is illustrative of this church's reputation for defending its ecumenical existence.[26]

Family is another factor keeping Huff's together. Many members attest to having Lutheran and Reformed sides to their families. In their church, one need not decide for one over the other. Resentment over the move thirty years ago to break up Union Churches stemmed in part from the damage such a break would do to interchurch families who had worshiped together for years. And, say some members, why should the community experienced with neighbors at work, school, leisure, be broken on Sunday for, of all things, worship? Why not together?

26. Huff's Union Church, Kropa, interview.

Admittedly, there have been some who have moved into the area, tried Huff's, and moved on. They needed the exact bearings of one tradition, not two. To those, members offer an understanding farewell. More incomprehensible, though, say long-time Huffites, are congregations—union or otherwise—who yell at one another over everything from carpet shade to theological nuance. "We've had some skirmishes," said one member, "but never anything like that."[27] Stubbornness is not always about holding ground as the one against the many, but as the many in unity against outside forces that would threaten unity.

"This church has made me more accepting, more universal, and more aware of other paths and possibilities," mused one member. "Why do we have this Chinese menu when we have one Lord?!"[28] he asked.

That said, there are ways to be grounded in one or the other tradition. Offering envelopes are filled out, designated to historic offerings for orphanages, missions, and other ministries in either the Evangelical Lutheran Church in America or the United Church of Christ. "You are both," Pastor Kropa tells her confirmands. "You have the best of all possible worlds."[29]

THE LONG GENERATION'S FUTURE

The "Save the Union" buttons of a few decades ago could still be worn in some quarters, where ecclesiastics puzzled by the longevity of these churches do not know quite what to make of them. These sentiments may even be found in some union congregations, or even among pastors who want to pull the opposite congregation toward the pastor's tradition, or, where one pastor of each denomination serve together but have not found ways to harmonize their ministries for the good of both congregations. Other pastors, enthusiastic for their union congregations, have gathered for annual retreats to share common concerns and frustrations. More often than not, their frustrations have to do with lack of understanding of their unique congregations on the part of respective judicatories.

Fortunately, there are ways, large and small, to continue to instruct the wider church on the historic witness of this form of grassroots ecumenism and to instill in the congregations themselves a deepening appreciation of the Union Church heritage. Jerusalem Western Salisbury Church, near Allentown, Pennsylvania, is a Union Church served by United Church of Christ

27. Huff's Union Church, group, interview.
28. Huff's Union Church, Moll, interview.
29. Huff's Union Church, Kropa, interview.

and Evangelical Lutheran Church in America clergypersons. Pastor Homer Royer notes that every Sunday's worship at Jerusalem Western includes the lighting of a unity candle by the pastors, with connections intended to the wedding context in which the symbol is often used. A Union Church trades on the marriage metaphor: two are one, yet they remain two in important ways. The individual theological gifts and practices are not extinguished, but allowed to stand together, just as, in marriage, the personhood and formative experiences of the spouses are not left behind for a blurred unity in a *tertium quid*.[30]

Pastor Jerel Gade of Saint Peter's Union Church, a few miles from Huff's in Macungie, Pennsylvania, is adamant that the union arrangement does not amount to a "community church," a term most union practitioners would strongly reject. "We want both traditions to live, not melt away."[31]

However, some see unionism as a stage—the step of a long generation— on the way to yet closer affiliation in dual and federated relationships, a step currently being taken by Huff's Church. Financial arrangements are most involved in making such a change, as the two congregations would move from two treasuries to one. In some Union churches, there are actually three incorporated entities: the congregations of both denominations, and the Union Church itself, all three having their own governance structures, treasurers, and bank accounts. In an email to the author, Pastor Kropa explained:

> For us, federation is when one congregation in the same building, and has gone through the legal process of becoming one legal entity.... At Huff's, it will mean we legally dissolve the ELCA and the UCC congregations, and have just one congregation, which will be fully bi-denominational. Federation is the final legal product of forming just one corporation to represent the congregation. Huff's has unified membership (everyone is a member of both ELCA and UCC) but has not yet unified its treasuries (we still operate with three treasuries, so we still need three sets of officers). In the not-too-far future, we hope to dissolve both the ELCA and UCC congregations, and operate with one corporation, one set of officers, one treasury, etc. and only then, will we be considered federated.

Unionism, here, is seen as the cooperation of two congregations in one facility. A "dual" arrangement is a step involving sharing of worship and clergy that invites consideration of the type of organic unity described above. It is a testament to Huff's tenacious commitment to ecumenism that it is approaching this step at this writing.

30. Huff's Union Church, Royer, interview.
31. Huff's Union Church, Gade, interview.

However, struggles that have dogged the union arrangement from colonial times are still in force in some places today, especially among clergy and synodical leaders who fear a dilution of traditions or who perceive confusion on the part of would-be parishioners, uneasy about "compromise," or the known quantity of a denominational identity. On the other hand, the late twentieth century ecumenical dialogues and agreements between Lutheran and Reformed families have added authority to common local endeavors. The cultural reasons for unionism among the Pennsylvania Dutch described earlier may have largely vanished, but the legacy is 250 years of ecumenical experience that, where successful, stands as a testament that (given favorable circumstances and willing participants) ecumenical shared ministry works.

PART II

Living Into Shared
Ministry Partnerships

6

Parish Life Cycles and Multi-Denominational Ministries

THE REV. DR. JAMES Reho is the Episcopal priest serving Lamb of God Church, a joint Evangelical Lutheran Church in America-Episcopal Church parish in Fort Myers, Florida. A scientist before seminary, Fr. Reho has an interest in evolutionary spirituality. He uses a scientific concept called "the hopeful monster" as an analogy for the ecumenical shared ministry parish concept. Fr. Reho said:

> In biology there will be, from time to time in a species, something called "the hopeful monster." The hopeful monster is a member of the tribe, but it is substantially different. The hopeful monster will—if it is successful—create a step-function change almost, in the gene pool of that population. So it ends up creating an impulse toward the future, or it dies; most hopeful monsters, they're going to die. A federated church is kind of an ecclesial hopeful monster. So it needs, I believe, a bit of a wide berth to be that hopeful monster. If what's happening isn't working well, it will die eventually. If what it's doing and experimenting with—and, of course, here you have to trust the clergy in charge that they are doing their best to represent these traditions authentically—but within this unique set of parameters, if that does thrive, it will offer back into each of the traditional judicatories a lot of wisdom at some point.[1]

---

1. Lamb of God Church, Reho, interview.

This chapter looks at the changes over time—the life cycle—of ecumenical shared ministry parishes. Drawing upon congregational life cycle studies,[2] we explore how these "hopeful monsters" have unique characteristics to bring to the congregational gene pool. We explore various ways in which these interchurch congregations are birthed, describe some of the issues that arise in mid-life, and address new opportunities that come with maturation and longevity in ministry. We also look at how they sometimes die, either of natural causes or by eradication by external forces. For each stage, we explore how these multi-denominational parishes are thriving and the challenges and conflicts they face.

In his booklet, *The Life Cycle of a Parish*, Martin Saarinen writes: "Given the dynamic quality of congregational life, change is the only constant. Congregations, at any given point in time, are in transition from one stage to another and factors characteristic of more than one stage will be comingled and in tension."[3] Change as the only constant is most certainly the case in ecumenical shared parish ministry.

BIRTH/INFANCY

There are three models by which multi-denominational parishes come into being. First is a parish that is birthed as a shared ministry, a church start that is designed to be intentionally ecumenical from its inception. Such parishes usually emerge in new communities, such as resource towns or the planned suburbs of growing cities. United Christian Parish (UCP) in Reston, Virginia, is a prime example of the latter. A suburb of Washington, DC, Reston is a planned community that was built in the 1960s to make housing, shopping, work, and other resident needs locally available with minimal transportation. This ecumenical parish was envisioned based on the then-thriving COCU (the Consultation on Church Union) multilateral ecumenical dialogue. United Christian Parish was, and is, one parish that was officially related to the United Church of Christ, the Christian Church (Disciples of Christ), the Presbyterian Church USA, and the United Methodist Church. Three church buildings were built initially, so for the first two decades the ministry was one congregation in three locations. Maintaining three properties proved to be unsustainable, so in the late 1990s the congregation sold two of the buildings, remodeled the third, and became one congregation in one location officially

2. Particularly Saarinen, *Life Cycle of a Congregation*.

3. Saarinen, *Life Cycle of a Congregation*, 7.

related to four denominations. (United Christian Parish is described in more detail in chapter 4.)

Denominations have discovered they can do more together in ethnic-specific ministries by pooling financial and personnel resources. For example, Episcopal priest Chantal McKinney received grants in 2016 from the Evangelical Lutheran Church in America and the Episcopal Church to establish a joint mission for Latinos and blacks in Winston-Salem, North Carolina. The Comunidad Amada de Cristo/Christ's Beloved Community is envisioned to be a congregation that is Episcopal-Lutheran, English-Spanish, and multicultural, focusing on neighborhood development, family, and community, and seeking to break down racial barriers through living and worshiping in community.

This approach to new ministries requires navigation of differing denominational approaches to mission. Planting new congregations in the Evangelical Lutheran Church in America is generally planned and funded at the national church level in consultation with the local synod, whereas in the Episcopal Church, new mission starts are planned and funded entirely by the local diocese. Coordinating these varying levels of judicatory responsibility adds a level of complexity to the planning and design process for an ecumenical parish. Birthing an ecumenical parish also requires identifying a clergy person who is comfortable serving multiple groups and empowering parishioners to develop a sense of belonging to these groups. And, as with all mission starts, adequate funding is often a key determiner as to whether a new parish survives and thrives, or not.

The second, and most common, birth narrative involves two (or more) established congregations of different denominations intentionally coming together to become an ecumenical shared parish. Merger for survival is a common theme. However, if survival is the only impetus, the new entity is probably as doomed as were the original parishes. A parishioner at Spirit of Grace in Hood River noted: "There are a lot of hospice churches. I like the ecumenical thing when it's an indicator that people are serious about what it means to be the church."[4] If two struggling communities of faith can capture a vision of the Holy Spirit doing a new thing, inspiring the people of God to create a new and renewed faith community in that place and time, then this "ecumenical thing" can be a creative and successful new venture.

Such ministries need a conviction that, to survive, they must come into a whole new way of being, stepping out together in faith. Sometimes this insight comes from within the parishes themselves, and parishioners and clergy initiate the merger. At other times, a judicatory leader has a vision for new ecumenical partnerships. ELCA Bishop Claire Burkat, says, "Ten years ago, it was

4. Spirit of Grace, Hood River, Siekkinen, interview.

all about property and buildings. This is an opportunity to cut through the old money and/or membership fights that divided us in typical suburban land-owning ministries. The ones we need to plant fast and furious are *these.* . . . Instead of waiting for everyone to agree on everything, can we just carve out a spot and be more experimental?"[5] When the judicatory leader is the initiator, he or she must have a willing partner in the other church judicatory. Both must work to help the local communities capture the vision.

The power dynamics of a merging group need judicatory attention as well. "I think the other thing that was underneath it, was power struggle," a lay member confessed. "People would be giving up power and control, and there was a lot of fear around that. 'What's going to happen if I am not in charge?' or 'I am diluting my authority and spreading it out to others who did not grow up like I did.' 'What is this going to mean?' The undercurrent of power, that was huge."[6] These power struggles have the potential to take place among clergy, parish staff, altar guilds, choirs, council members, and informal lay leaders. Anywhere there is leadership is also the potential for power-based conflict that can thwart the formation of the ministry in its earliest stages.

The creation of this form of ecumenical shared parish is usually char-acterized as a merger, symbolized by a new name for the new combined ecu-menical entity. However, at the Church of the Nativity and Holy Comforter, the priest says: "We don't use the word 'merge'—that implies that someone loses something. We use 'partner' or 'create' instead."[7] Regardless of termi-nology, the congregations involved face the challenges of transition: finding a new, multi-denominational identity and determining how to handle building issues. Often one congregation is leaving a building behind, requiring pas-toral grief work with that group and Christian hospitality on the part of the receiving congregation. The group remaining in its building must welcome the other group in—along with all their church possessions—and share the space with the newcomers. "When the moving van came [delivering the other parish's belongings], it got real," Fr. Lucas says.[8] But hospitality, even radical hospitality, is not enough to sustain an ecumenical shared parish for the long haul. Hospitality has to evolve into a sense of common mission and mutuality in ministry.

As ecumenical parishes are formed, clergy and lay leaders must be at-tentive to the emotional realities around grief and loss, "it produced a kind

5. Burkat, Lutheran Episcopal Coordinating Committee meeting.

6. Spirit of Grace, Hood River, Chenoweth, interview.

7. Church of the Nativity and Holy Comforter, Lucas, interview with the National Lutheran Episcopal Coordinating Committee.

8. Church of the Nativity and Holy Comforter, Lucas, interview.

of polarity, anxiety pulling in both directions,"[9] one pastor observes. The Lutheran pastor in the Cedarcroft partnership, David Eisenhuth, was intentional about helping the Lutheran parishioners deal with their grief over giving up their long-term building and moving into the Episcopalians' space. In parallel, the Episcopal priest, Fr. Lucas, talked with the Episcopalians about the Lutheran grief they should expect. The Lutherans held a service on the eve of Reformation Sunday as a liturgical and spiritual good-bye to the building. In the liturgy, they moved around the sanctuary, saying good-bye and thanking God for each piece of liturgical furniture: the altar, the font, the pulpit. They invited the Episcopalians to attend on their final service on Reformation Sunday. Parishioners of both denominations later described that service as having the feel of a wake: telling funny stories, laughter and tears together. The grief was manageable because the emotional preparation had already been done. The following Sunday, All Saints Day, was the inaugural service of the new ecumenical parish, held in its new home in the Episcopal parish. The clergy expected ninety in attendance; actual attendance was 130.

A significant challenge of such a merger is the inevitable change in worship practices and patterns, discussed in other chapters. It involves the nitty-gritty of merging altar guilds and communion elders. When the Lutherans in Baltimore brought over their communion trays and sterling silver chalice, the Episcopal altar guild immediately polished it, and then said, "What are we going to do with these communion trays?" Working out the logistics of communion distribution between the Episcopal common cup tradition and the Lutheran trays of individual communion cups required diplomacy among themselves and in the local bishops' offices. The two groups also discussed how they would merge their kitchen equipment and food traditions. Church leaders report that openness, intentionality, and laughter were the keys to success.

Merging staff, especially when layoffs must happen due to duplication of roles, can be painful. In the new Cedarcroft partnership, for example, the choir instantly jumped from six members to fifteen. However, the inevitable loss of one beloved choir director and the resulting adjustment to the style of the other was difficult for the newly merged choir in its first year.

Even the merger of two parish Facebook pages can turn out to be more complicated than expected. The clergy in Cedarcroft felt this social media move was important symbolically: both to retain the history and photos of the congregations prior to the partnership and to establish a social media identity for the new parish entity. They ran into an unexpected ten-day waiting period because they wanted to use a new name for the merged Facebook

9. Spirit of Grace, Hood River, Richards, interview.

page. However, almost immediately the ecumenical parish had 379 Facebook followers, some of them new followers resulting from the publicity about the ecumenical partnership.

A third way in which a multi-denominational parish may come into being is when a one-denomination parish receives a mission group from a different denomination. This was the model that birthed the Lutheran-Roman Catholic Mission of the Atonement parish in Beaverton, Oregon (described in chapter 3). This is also the case for Epiphany Lutheran-Episcopal parish in Marina, California. The challenges of this model include the unequal partnership in money and/or in property, as well as the lack of parity in status as a congregation and in relationship with the two judicatories involved. In Epiphany's case, for example, the Episcopal part of the partnership is a mission of a separate Episcopal parish in nearby Carmel, whereas the Lutheran part of the partnership has no third parish entity involved in its governance or decision-making.

No matter how the "hopeful monster" comes into being, the deepest reality is the call to each clergyperson and each parishioner to follow the Spirit's prompting for a new parish life, a new, shared journey that will be different from what came before. As the Rev. Stephen Bancroft says, "It has to do with giving up one's sense of institutional connections and willingness to say, 'Okay, I am here for God, not for a diocese, not for congregation, but for where God is going to lead us.' To put that at the beginning and the end of the whole thing."[10] The hope, excitement, and the vision of this new entity carry these parishes through the hard work of federation and into a new identity.

ADOLESCENCE

The keys to transitioning into a permanent identity as an ecumenical shared parish are finding a common mission, establishing financial viability, and developing programs. The challenges that Spirit of Grace United Methodist-Evangelical Lutheran Church in America parish in Hood River, Oregon faced, around settling into and claiming its new identity were described in chapter 1. In Hood River, as we noted, members found their common purpose through building and running the community food bank.

St. Peter's Ecumenical Church, the Anglican-Lutheran-United Church shared ministry at Slave Lake, Alberta, emerged in the mid-1970s, but even by the early 1980s had not quite found its feet. As Heather Labrie, a long-time lay leader, described it: "During these teenage years we found we suffered the

10. Spirit of Grace, West Bloomfield, Bancroft, interview.

pangs of not being accepted by our peers and parents. We were definitely a problem for our respective judicatories." It was only when two "wonderful bishops"—Anglican Gary Woolsey and Lutheran Bob Jacobsen—caught the vision, saw ecumenism "positively," and worked together to assist the congregation that St. Peter's landed on firmer ground. By the early 1990s, she could report: "Today . . . we have achieved some maturity and are feeling good about ourselves."[11] In 2012, the congregation consecrated a new church building.

At Spirit of Grace ELCA-Episcopal parish in West Bloomfield, Michigan, the merger process went smoothly. More challenging were the questions around the new ecumenical parish's mission identity, as they attempted to merge their differing approaches to outreach. The original Lutheran group was neighborhood-based, reaching out to the community immediately surrounding the church and working with the neighborhood school district in suburban Detroit. Being known to the neighborhood was a high value for this group, and they feared that moving away from neighborhood outreach as the focus of their ministries would change their identity. "I did not want to let our reputation die as a community church," said the outreach coordinator.[12] The Episcopal group within the parish was accustomed to a more episodic model and had focused their mission work on service projects in inner-city Detroit. This group felt the city had the greatest need and thus their efforts could have the greatest impact there. Determining what programs were sustainable and which were expendable was central to moving forward into a new merged entity.

PRIME/MATURITY

The challenges of an ecumenical shared parish at mid-life often center on transitions of key players: clergy, judicatory leaders, lay leaders. The loss of a charismatic leader can require the group to revisit identity questions and develop new, shared leadership models. Often there is time to plan carefully for these transitions; other times not. Holy Apostles Episcopal-Roman Catholic parish in Virginia Beach (described in chapter 3), faced a sudden and unexpected clergy transition in 2012 when the Roman Catholic bishop unexpectedly removed their long-time Roman Catholic priest, and then again in June 2016, when their long-term Episcopal priest, the Rev. Michael Ferguson, died suddenly of a heart attack while on vacation.

11. Heather Labrie, "Tragedies, Illness, and Disappointments Draw People Together: St. Peter's Ecumenical Church," in Barker, *Lively Option*, 21–22.

12. Spirit of Grace, West Bloomfield, James Bugg, interview.

Other clergy transitions happen more slowly but with no less turmoil for the parish. Sunriver Christian Fellowship (described in chapter 1) realizes that its founding and long-term clergyperson, Episcopal priest Nancy McGrath-Green, will be required by her denomination to retire from full-time ministry within the next few years. The associate pastor will also soon retire. Though the parish is now a multi-denominational mix in membership (with only forty percent of the membership identifying as either Lutheran or Episcopal), the parish is officially a joint ELCA-Episcopal one. Thus, the parish bylaws state that the call process will be under the jurisdiction of the local ELCA bishop, and the parish will need to seek either a Lutheran or an Episcopal clergyperson. Some parish members believe that the bylaws ought to be changed to allow for a wider, more ecumenical search, asking, "Why not search for the right clergy of any denominational brand, the person who best fits the ecumenical profile of the parish?"

Changes of judicatory leadership can also pose a difficulty for ecumenical parishes. The formation and support of a multi-denominational ministry is often the product of two local bishops working closely together on a venture to which they both are deeply committed. The shift from a supportive ecumenical bishop to a traditionalist, denominationally-focused bishop can be difficult for these parishes. Holy Apostles [Episcopal-Roman Catholic] in Virginia Beach is an example.

Shared ministries tend to attract parishioners deeply committed to this model. These parishes are often located in vacation areas or rural regions with lower mobility. Thus, they tend to have stable membership patterns. By mid-life, the challenge often becomes a congregation aging in place, and parish leaders must redefine mission as capabilities for mission change and physical infirmities increase. Outreach to a new generation also becomes a challenge. The priest at Sunriver Christian Fellowship in Sunriver, Oregon, a resort community, said that aging is the biggest challenge facing the congregation. "We get older every year," she observed, "and unless we can get some newer members coming in, the impact of our ministry will diminish because we simply, physically cannot do what we once did. We have to remember that it is as important to love our own as it to love our neighbor and to make sure we are there for them. Their needs become dramatic and huge, understandably so, and take a lot of appropriate energy from us. We are all on that journey."[13] Ultimately, it is the radical hospitality in Christ that people experience as visitors and as long-term parishioners that is the key to success in ministry.

Lamb of God, an ELCA-Episcopal joint parish in Ft Myers, Florida, is a prime example of a mature shared ministry parish that has weathered the

13. Sunriver Christian Fellowship, McGrath-Green, interview.

challenges of life stages. Lamb of God is one of the oldest and largest Lutheran-Episcopal partnerships in the United States. Formed in 2000 when the nearby Episcopal parish (St. Joseph's) had a crisis and Lamb of God Lutheran Church welcomed them in, it was a guest/host relationship at first. When the congregation officially federated in 2004, it became a fully joint parish incorporated as Lamb of God and governed with a constitution and bylaws for the ecumenical entity.

Currently forty percent of the congregational membership at Lamb of God is seasonal, i.e., those members summer in another geographic location. Although the congregation is largely made up of older adults, mostly retirees, the parish is committed to being multigenerational. "I don't want a ghettoized church," Fr. Reho said, "I want the church to look like the kingdom of God."[14] Members belong to both the ELCA and the Episcopal Church. Of those who currently attend worship, forty percent are ELCA Lutheran; forty percent are ex-Roman Catholic or ex-Baptist; and twenty percent are Episcopalians. On Palm Sunday 2016, worship attendance was 330. On an ordinary Sunday in season, the church averages 230 at the main service, and fifteen to thirty at the early service. In summer, which is low season in this resort community, attendance averages 150 at the main service and ten to twelve at early service. When asked, "What keeps you here?" members responded, "relationships—the people, the clergy." Father Reho describes the parish as "a missional church doing outreach in both justice and charity work." "People here know and believe that the church exists for the sake of the world," he says.[15] A recent Lenten study series, "Jesus as Justice," addressed sex trafficking, hunger, poverty in the community, and genetically modified organisms.

Lamb of God's challenges are those of any parish in a resort community: the seasonality of part-time members, communicating with members while they are away, the gulf between the "haves" and "have-nots" in the community, and a church building surrounded by gated housing communities. But Lamb of God has weathered one of the major challenges of established long-term multi-denominational parishes: the successful transition from the founding clergy person, who was deeply personally identified with the parish, to a new clergy person with a new approach. Establishing a healthy ongoing ministry under next generation leadership is essential in congregations in their prime.

Lutheran pastor Walter Fohs, the long-term senior clergy person of Lamb of God parish, was known widely throughout the church for this ministry. Speaking about Lamb of God parish to the Lutheran Episcopal Coordinating Committee in 2011, Pastor Fohs expressed how much he valued the

14. Lamb of God Church, Reho, interview.
15. Lamb of God Church, Reho, interview.

ecumenical nature of the church and also his fear that the parish's ecumenical identity might be too closely identified with him as an individual. His great hope, he said, was that the parish would transition well upon his retirement. Three years later, the parish has successfully moved from a rather informal, Hawaiian-shirt-style Lutheran pastor to an Episcopal priest who vests in a cope. In reflecting upon the success of the transition, Fr. James Reho, the Episcopal priest, credits an intentional interim clergyperson who prepared the congregation to be open to new styles of ministry. Fr. Reho's sense of self-awareness was also crucial. He said, "Whenever something would change, I've tried to do my best to affirm what was and why that was of value, as well as why the change is of value now."[16]

Identity questions also surface at mid-life for these parishes. At Lamb of God, some are asking the question, "Are we Lutheran-Episcopal, or something entirely different?" This question arose at the Board of Trustees' outreach conversation. "We want to use different words so we don't fall back on 'Lutheran-Episcopal,'" a member said. "Those words are too loaded with old concepts. We need to put those aside for words that people will find more intriguing."[17] Parish size is also a mid-life issue. One trustee observed that Lamb of God "is an awkward size: large enough to have lots of activities but not large enough to programmatize everything." Another mused: "How big do we want to be?"[18]

Lamb of God parish is a model for the kind of evaluation, self-analysis, and intentional planning necessary for continued congregational growth and maturation in faith and mission. They have embarked upon what Fr. Reho calls a "reformulation time," looking at "missional reformulation, liturgical reformulation, and denominational reformulation,"[19] as they wrestle with parish identity for the next phase of life together.

DEATH—AND RESURRECTION

Ecumenical shared parishes do not die any more frequently than any other parish. However, they do come under distinct stresses that can impair their survival. When these parishes die, they usually do so because external factors were hostile or unsupportive. Most, like parishes across the United States and Canada, die a natural death through aging and de-population of their area. Others, however, are afflicted by matters particular to their ecumenical

---

16. Lamb of God Church, Reho, interview.

17. Lamb of God Church, Frye, Board of Trustees conversation.

18. Lamb of God Church, Whitehouse and Vath, Board of Trustees conversation.

19. Reho, PowerPoint.

sharing. In the 1970s, many Anglican Church of Canada-United Church of Canada parishes were formed in expectation of an impending merger of the two denominations into one denomination. Judicatories instigated many of these, not always with sufficient intentionality and commitment from the congregations. Some congregations then fell apart when the anticipated denominational merger did not take place as expected. Others were unwound by bishops who were hostile to the proposed union.

In 1981, an Anglican bishop ended Anglican participation in a long-standing United Church of Canada-Anglican Church of Canada parish, St. Paul's-St. Cuthbert's Church in Princeton, British Columbia, when the pastoral relationship with the congregation's United Church minister broke down. The Anglicans were upset and refused to leave; they just kept going to worship at that parish. Eventually, a successor Anglican bishop encouraged them to continue. Now, even though it is not officially an ecumenical shared parish, it is a United Church of Canada parish with a significant population of embedded Anglicans. The current Anglican bishop happily visits the parish annually. Persistence—with a touch of defiance—won.

Another shared ministry ended in 2005 when a long-term Roman Catholic-Anglican Church of Canada ecumenical parish on an island off the coast of British Columbia, was unilaterally terminated by the new Roman Catholic bishop. The communities were heartbroken, as they had formed deep bonds. The Anglicans knew they needed a new sharing arrangement to continue their own ministry, but they also needed time to grieve the loss of their long-term Roman Catholic partners. Just over a decade later, they entered joyfully into a new shared ministry with the United Church parish, creating one church with a new name: Christ Church Gabriola—"a Collaborative Anglican-United Church open to all."[20] "We know that we have passed from death to life because we love one another," the author of 1 John reminded the early Christians (1 John 3:14). Such can be the story of multi-denominational parishes.

Each of these parishes moves through a life cycle just as individuals do, and every parish must re-claim and re-interpret its unique parish identity in every stage of life. Multi-denominational parishes have a vocation for shared witness and a commitment to ministry to the diversity of the Christian family that is a model for the future. The priest of Sunriver Christian Fellowship summed up the enthusiasm of many of those who serve in shared ministry contexts,

> I am convinced that ecumenical ministry is the wave of the future.
> It has no other option but that. We cannot afford to have churches

20. Christ Church Gabriola website.

on every street corner, and they are all fighting the light bill and the roof replacement and the parking lot re-pavement. Why spend your dollars there when the human family is crying out for help? We have a panorama on Sunday mornings here that paints different denominations coming together, all bringing their piece of the truth behind this one altar, saying to our congregation: Look at this incredible scenery of God's great family and how God in the Spirit has moved through time. We can learn from the wisdom of each tradition, sharing our own, not feeling intimidated by difference, but celebrating difference, meeting at the table, receiving the spiritual food, how you want to translate that of Jesus himself coming into ourselves. If we can carry out that mission to go forth out the door and serve our neighbor together as a much bigger body of people, with many more dollars that we can share, and many more energy cells which can kick into gear to help the neighbor, then we are much better for it. Jesus delights in it. I think God is thrilled. I think it is without a doubt the answer to church in the future.[21]

The church needs more such ministries—the hopeful monsters.

---

21. Sunriver Christian Fellowship, McGrath-Green, interview.

7

"They Turned to Face Us"
Worshiping Together

ON A WARM JUNE Sunday, the congregation of Deer Park United Church held one final brief service in their former building—majestic, historic, but unaffordable—in uptown Toronto, then headed down the street and around the corner to Calvin Presbyterian Church, with whom they had agreed, after several years of searching for a future, to share life, worship, and ministry. Their minister, the Rev. Marie Goodyear, describes the event:

> We had a short de-sanctification service (the big farewell had been the week before); then we walked down St Clair Avenue and up to Calvin, led by three people: one carrying the cross from the communion table, one carrying the chalice, and one carrying the Christ candle. The rest of us followed behind. We had a little service at the Calvin doorway, and knocked on the door. They opened the door, and we walked in. The Calvin people were there; they were singing a hymn, but rather than facing the front, they had turned to face us as they sang. Also, they were standing off to the sides of the centre aisle so that we could go into the pews without climbing over anyone. It was the most incredibly welcoming way of doing it.[1]

Worship lies at the beating heart of the Christian community. Christians through the centuries have gifted to the church liturgies, rites, and symbols that express the inexpressible—awe, joy, sorrow, fear, commitment. Liturgical

---

1. Deer Park and Calvin, Goodyear, interview.

theologian Aidan Kavanagh famously wrote, "A liturgy of Christians is nothing less than the way a redeemed world is, so to speak, done."[2] Inter-church congregations have the opportunity to hold fast to tradition and to create liturgy afresh as they practice the "redeemed world" once more, Sunday by Sunday. The Deer Park and Calvin congregations recreated age-old rituals—processing, knocking on the church door to ask for hospitality, singing, turning to greet the newcomers. However, these ancient gestures were also new actions for a new relationship. Ecumenical shared ministry is full of such thrilling liturgical moments.

Of course, worship in ecumenical ministries is also about the week-by-week experience of the Christian year, and every congregation practices its denominational liturgies with its own unique flavor. Ecumenical shared ministries bring denominational and local norms and expectations to the relationship. When parishioners ask, "What will I have to give up in this inter-church ministry?" their fears often center on sacrificing beloved aspects of their weekly worship life. However, the experience of shared worship often *becomes* the beloved aspect of a shared ministry. As a member of a three-denomination congregation puts it: "In all three traditions, I find such richness. There is nothing in any one of the liturgies that provides any reason to reject it. Everything I would look for is there."[3]

Ecumenical developments of the late twentieth century helped to pave the way for multi-denominational congregational worship. Formal ecumenical dialogues brought Christians to remarkable convergences on baptism and the Eucharist. Liturgical theologians began to take seriously the early church's worship rites, and most mainstream denominations took hold of the gathering/word/table pattern that emerged from those investigations, along with a renewed interest in the seasons of the church year. Denominations, even those with deep ties to one worship book (such as the *Book of Common Prayer*) developed worship books and resources reflecting the "ecumenical liturgical convergence" as well as their own contexts. The Consultation on Common Texts brought the Revised Common Lectionary to the churches, and most mainstream churches in North America began to use it—with varying degrees of rigor. Seminaries began to teach worship in this more ecumenically grounded way. These advances did not homogenize worship across the churches. Rather, they allowed Christians to recognize their own faith and liturgical expressions in the worship of others, and so to open themselves to what might happen in multi-denominational ministry. In this spirit, the liturgy becomes not so much an obstacle to surmount as an opportunity for

2. Kavanagh, *Liturgical Theology*, 100.

3. St. Peter's Ecumenical Church, Prévost, interview.

98

the congregation to deepen its awareness of what is possible in the worship of God. The worship experience becomes an occasion to receive the gifts of other traditions at their most profound: in the words and actions, the song and silence of the community gathered in praise and prayer.

This chapter describes ways to approach the worship life of multi-denominational congregations, looking first at a process for helping determine how worship might unfold, and then at the patterns that emerge. We discuss briefly the distinct case of shared ministries with Roman Catholic partners; finally, we consider the celebration of special rites, particularly baptism and confirmation, as places of unique challenges and opportunities for ecumenical ministries.

PROCESS: "WE HAVE DONE A LOT OF LAUGHING"

An Anglican priest serving a four-denomination parish in Tumbler Ridge, British Columbia, in the 1990s, writes of beginning his ministry among them:

> When it came to designing worship services for this congregation, I asked them what they wanted. The reply I received was, "Do whatever you want and we will tell you what we like and don't like." Not much guidance to a man used to a book where everything is laid out for him. Discovering when people stand and sit, what they like to sing or how the last minister did things were all part of the challenge. I thought I was such a non-traditional. We have done a lot of laughing over this in the last few months.[4]

Worship, while both central and complicated in multi-denominational ministry, has the great advantage of mutability. Unlike decisions to keep or sell a building, or to determine who will be the paid minister, a congregation can alter the practice of worship. Those entering into a shared ministry agreement need to know their traditions will be honored and their worship will reflect their faith and commitments. However, if some aspect of worship life fails to satisfy, it can change. Shared ministry congregations do not necessarily know what will work best when they first come together. Some will assume a rotation among the liturgies of their denominations from the outset. Others—particularly those that include denominations without a firmly fixed liturgy—might employ a variation of the Tumbler Ridge model: "Do what you want, and we'll tell you what we like." However, it can be helpful and mutually enriching to dig a little deeper together.

---

4. Brent Neumann, "A Unique Sense of Grace: St. Paul's, Tumbler Ridge, B.C.," in Barker, *Lively Option*, 94.

Based on a chart prepared by Churches Together in England, which facilitates and supports multi-denominational congregations, it can be helpful for such congregations, and for clergy and judicatories who will serve and support them, to ask a few questions about liturgy in their participating denominations. With people grouped by denomination, they can ask themselves questions, which they then "map" for one another in a chart format.

Who Decides What Happens in Worship in Your Congregation?

This is a crucial question, as the answers will differ significantly across denominations. For most Anglicans/Episcopalians, for example, the national church authorizes worship books, and the bishop grants approvals for exceptions; local congregations make their worship decisions within those parameters. In the United Church of Canada, by contrast, the national church produces resources, but the local congregation takes all worship decisions, preferably through an active worship committee working with the minister. Each denomination will offer a slightly different response to that question, and there is no doubt these differences in authority structures for worship decisions can be a source of anxiety and tension. Nevertheless, *knowing* what they are can also help diffuse and depersonalize worship conflict.

What Would You Name as the Essentials for any Worship Experience?

This is an important step, as it asks people to reflect on the meaning of worship in the context of their tradition. It also takes them into that ecumenically shared space that promises to honor their deepest commitments, while asking them to set priorities. Some ecumenical theologians call this exercise the creation of a "hierarchy of truths."

What Would Need to Be in Place Regularly in Worship, if Not Always?

This question can elicit interesting responses, including corporate confession, chanted psalms, passing the peace, and "children's time." These elements are still important to weave into the worship fabric of the congregation, but how often is more negotiable than the items named in the previous section.

What Are the "Sticking Points" Around Liturgy in Your Context?

This question acknowledges that no denomination is without internal differences around worship. It asks people to be honest about the family squabbles they bring into the inter-church relationship. "Inclusive" language, music styles, which "setting," which prayer book—all these are debated internally in some denominations. Encouraging humility in presenting the foibles and gifts of one's own tradition (and the trust that such candor can engender) this question can also help preclude generalizations. Not "All Lutherans" may behave in the way an Episcopalian might suppose.

Do Any "Key Themes" Emerge from These Responses?

This question is the result of an insight by a Lutheran minister, the Rev. Brian Krushel, who was participating in this exercise with clergy and lay leaders from four denominations.[5] He suggested words that captured the main thrust of each tradition's responses: "prayer" for Anglicans, "preaching" for Lutherans, and so on. The whole group should share this question as they reflect on the completed worship chart. By coming up with "key themes" together, people can begin to understand one another's most basic faith needs and desires, a way to build respect and trust.

This mapping exercise does not resolve worship dilemmas or determine how a multi-denominational congregation should proceed. Rather, it offers raw data out of which an ecumenical ministry can build (or rebuild, or continue to celebrate) its liturgical life. It fosters knowledge and understanding of unfamiliar traditions. The exercise can serve as a reminder that everyone—even those whose denominations do not prescribe worship texts—brings to liturgy the treasured ways of praying in community. It also offers clues for the compromises required to worship together. The Rev. Leigh Sinclair describes decisions around worship at St. Peter's, Slave Lake, an Anglican/Lutheran/United Church congregation.

> Sometimes you need to make a choice. Whoever cares the least makes the change. United Church members are not offended by standing for the reading of the Gospel, so we do. Anglicans at St.

5. Preparing for Ecumenical Ministries course at the Sorrento Centre, British Columbia (July 2013).

Peter's are not offended if there is grape juice as well as wine on the communion table, and United Church people are totally offended if there is *not* grape juice on the table.[6]

We thus come to multi-denominational worship with respect, with gentleness, and with the indulgent laughter that comes from trying to get it right.

PATTERNS OF WORSHIP

Over the decades, multi-denominational congregations have practiced a variety of worship patterns, including the denominational liturgy of the pastor, with visiting clergy or judicatories supplying services in the other denomination(s) upon occasion. Currently, most shared ministries either rotate denominational liturgies, or use a "blended" liturgy reflecting the worship of the participating denominations. Some employ a combination of rotation and blended worship. Others add "pastor's choice" or a children's liturgy to the rotation, e.g., on every month with a fifth Sunday. There is no one "correct" or "better" pattern; each has unique gifts and challenges.

Rotating Denominational Liturgies

Most ecumenical shared ministries begin their lives together by rotating their liturgies. Our research suggests that more than half of multi-denominational congregations in the United States and Canada continue to worship with a rotational pattern, with occasional blended or special services. This pattern illustrates beautifully what many ecumenists see as an important development in the quest for Christian unity; namely, it demonstrates that coming together in one body does not obliterate the distinctiveness of our gifts. It maintains "unity in legitimate diversity," a favorite phrase of contemporary ecumenists, who point out that since earliest times Christians have wrestled with ways to accommodate different expressions and understandings of the faith.[7] The practice of rotating liturgies involves an acknowledgment, essential to the functioning of a multi-denominational ministry, that the worship of the "other," while perhaps neither preferred nor even, at first, comprehensible, has integrity.

Accepting the legitimacy of one another's worship does not make it easy to worship together initially. The formation of a shared ministry, or whenever

6. St. Peter's Ecumenical Church, Sinclair, interview.

7. For example, *Church: Towards a Common Vision*, par. 28–30.

a new member or clergyperson joins the community, can be a time of disorientation. "I was truly lost on the Lutheran and the Anglican Sundays," says Marge Procyshyn, a United Church member at St. Peter's Ecumenical Church, in Slave Lake.[8] One minister commented that it took four months to feel at ease with the liturgy of the other denomination.[9] A United Church minister, serving Anglican/United churches on Vancouver Island in the late 1960s, described his experience of ministering with Anglicans.

> They worked hard for about a year to accept me as a minister, to get over their emotional reactions to how I did an Anglican service. I suppose all of us [were] learning to trust each other, and in that time, I can remember things that were hurtful; you really had to learn almost instantly to forgive people for things.[10]

That same minister also recounted how his experience evolved. After "about a year and a half, I understood it. . . . It had become, I suppose, enough a part of me that my worship just flowed with it. I had just become bi-liturgical, really . . . genuinely worshiping with the Anglican liturgy."[11]

To become "bi-liturgical" (or "multi-liturgical") is a challenge and a gift. Not only the clergy, but music ministers and those who assist in the liturgy also need to learn to speak more than one liturgical language. Newcomers need gentle schooling in multiple rites. However, most worshipers experience being "bi-liturgical" as enriching, and even a powerful spiritual experience. Without losing one's own faith expression, one finds another one and, with it, new ways to encounter the holy. Speaking more than one language not only opens new worlds to the speaker, it also, scientists suggest, may shape the brain in ways that make it more creative and flexible.[12] People in shared ministries enjoy similar experiences. The woman who reported being initially "lost" in other liturgies now does not even bother to check to see what the service will be before heading off to church. "You get used to it. You don't know what it's going to be; it's never humdrum!"[13] It also helps Christians to resist idolatry of their own tradition. The notion that there may be more than one legitimate way to pray in turn helps to attract persons of denominations other than the official participants in the ministry. Said one such person, "Here we

---

8. St. Peter's Ecumenical Church, Procyshyn, interview.

9. Anonymous respondent to ESM survey.

10. Holmes, Interview for "Heritage Alive Program."

11. Holmes, Interview for "Heritage Alive Program."

12. See, for example, Anne Merritt, "Why Learn a Foreign Language?"

13. St. Peter's Ecumenical Church, Procyshyn, interview.

are all accepted unconditionally as the people of God. . . . Everyone is welcome at the table."[14]

Rotational liturgies present challenges beyond learning the rites. The congregation may need to own multiple sets of worship and music books and supplemental resources. There may be limits to the diversity based on one denomination's "essentials." An obvious example occurs in a shared ministry involving a Christian Church (Disciples of Christ) partner. Disciples must celebrate Holy Communion weekly. To enter into ecumenical shared ministry with Disciples means the service must include communion, regardless of whose order is used on a given Sunday. Where there is an Anglican or Episcopalian partner, the bishop reserves the right to license the clergy to perform the sacraments. Many bishops will not license a minister from a Reformed or other non-episcopal tradition, even in an interdenominational context. This licensing requirement can cause frustrations—both for clergy who struggle to make Anglican worship meaningful ("I find the Anglican Service of the Word a bit thin for a Sunday morning," said one United Church minister)[15] and for congregants who dislike waiting for a visiting clergyperson to preside at the Eucharist in their own tradition.

A final challenge is the question of indifference. The notion that North American Christians inhabit a post-denominational age can lead multi-denominational worshipers to ask why they need to protect their separate traditions so elaborately. However, those who have committed to the rotational model are clear in defending it. Leigh Sinclair observed, "Whenever someone says, 'It doesn't matter,' [using each denomination's liturgy] I say to that person, 'Really? It *really* doesn't matter?' And they say, 'No, you're right. If my Grandma was going to come to worship, it would matter to her, so it matters to me.'"[16]

"Blended" Liturgies

Few multi-denominational ministries set out to worship with a "blended" liturgy. However, even in a congregation with a commitment to rotating denominational services, blending breaks out. The "gorgeous" Lenten prayers in the Anglican Book of Alternative Services (a Canadian resource) invite their use every week in Lent. The Lutheran sung Gospel acclamation is so compelling it becomes a weekly norm. As François Prévost puts it: "There

14. St. Peter's Ecumenical Church, Prévost, interview.

15. Anonymous respondent to ESM survey.

16. St. Peter's Ecumenical Church, Sinclair, interview.

is borrowing, but in a positive sense—the borrowing that happens between friends. You have a different way of cooking potatoes, and I like your potatoes, so I might start cooking them that way too."[17] Such borrowing helps to give multi-denominational congregations some weekly continuity, unity within the diversity. Innovation also occurs as congregations develop new worship styles within their multi-denominational partnership. Awit Marcelino, a lay worship leader at Broadway Disciples United Church in Winnipeg noted, "We changed things as we grew. We didn't have a praise band in any of our [partnering] congregations. That's been new to all of us."[18] As with long-married couples, long-standing ecumenical partners can begin to resemble one another.

Apart from the natural liturgical sharing that occurs in multi-denominational ministry, there is also the impetus to worship with one liturgy, embracing all participating traditions. This impulse can emerge in unexpected ways. The Rev. Ray Cuthbert described what happened in the early, negotiating phase among the three congregations forming Broadway Disciples United Church.

> Part of what we did in the initial stage was to invite people of all three to experience worship in each other's setting. We wound up with the St. Stephen's Broadway service being on Palm Sunday. Bob [United Church minister] suggested that instead of just doing a United Church liturgy, why don't we build the service together? It was inspiring. We did a palm procession all around the sanctuary, and from that day to this it's the best service that happens each year in this congregation. We knew we didn't want to wait; we wanted to worship together like that every week.[19]

Sometimes it is the congregation members themselves who desire to worship in a blended style. They have worked hard to overcome obstacles, to become a new creation within the Body of Christ—a foretaste, perhaps, of Christian unity to come. They want their worship to reflect their deep and mutual belonging. Other times, it is the pastor who feels called to shape an experimental blended or common liturgy for the congregation. However it happens, congregations need to approach the aspiration to worship with a blended liturgy with care. Congregational leaders and indeed members need to be supportive. Provisions need to be in place for occasional denominational services. Where one or more of the participating denominations has its liturgies approved by a judicatory, the pastor and/or council needs to consult with

17. St. Peter's Ecumenical Church, Prévost interview.
18. Broadway Disciples United, Marcelino, interview.
19. Broadway Disciples United, Cuthbert, interview.

that person or body. This is one of those "limit-testing" moments in ecumenical ministry, and it requires the caution and forethought that generally accompany successful liminal innovations.

"Blended" may not be the ideal name for such liturgies, as it evokes the notion of taking the worship books and set orders, throwing them into a blender, and letting a set of sharp blades shred them into some new concoction. In fact, the process requires a deep awareness of the underlying structure of the traditions involved. The Rev. Ann Salmon, a Lutheran (ELCA and ELCIC) pastor who served two Anglican/Lutheran congregations in different parts of Canada, uses the language of "ordo": discovering the relationship of all parts of worship to one another. When one discerns this relationship, she argues, one discerns a root "ordo" out of which that denomination's worship arises.[20] Her method represents a deepening of the "key theme" exercise discussed in the first part of this chapter.

To create a warrant for a common liturgy for her congregation, Salmon considered the *ordo* of two resources. She worked with *Evangelical Lutheran Worship* (the primary worship resource for Lutherans in the ELCA and the ELCIC), and the *Book of Alternative Services*, prepared for and sanctioned by the Anglican Church of Canada as a book of contemporary rites intended to stand in continuity with the *Book of Common Prayer*. While they hold much in common, Salmon determined the Lutheran book represents an "Ordo of Grace" while the Anglican represents an "Ordo of Life." Any common liturgy would have to take these distinctive approaches into account. She concluded:

> The use of these ordos in a blended way in Anglican Lutheran shared ministry makes not only for an interesting theological conversation, but also for creative and beautiful worship. When ordos of grace and life abide with each other, and the people of God who love these languages of faith become fluent in each other's languages, the result is a new and very powerful way to speak and to live God's love in the world.[21]

WORSHIPING WITH ROMAN CATHOLIC PARTNERS

As noted in chapter 3, significant challenge confronts worshiping shared ministries with Roman Catholic partners. Their weekly worship must reckon with Roman Catholic theology around intercommunion. Without discounting the powerful convergences among Christians about the meaning and celebration

---

20. Salmon, "Effect of Worship," 12.

21. Salmon, "Effect of Worship," 21.

of the Eucharist, Roman Catholics understand intercommunion to be reserved for the day when the churches are in visible full communion—united in all aspects of faith and order,[22] while Protestants and Anglicans carry various, but more "open," understandings of the Eucharistic table. Multi-denominational ministries that involve Roman Catholic partners must reckon with it, and they do, with enormous grace. They share as much of the liturgical life as they can. Chapter 3 described these unique and ongoing worshiping arrangements as they unfolded in two American congregations. Both congregations find ways to be together for the Service of the Word, and to separate as gently as possible for the service of the table, making present in their worship their yearning for that day of visible unity and full communion.

A third Eucharistic experiment involving Roman Catholics began on Canada's Pacific Rim in the 1970s, "The Port Alice Liturgy." As part of a sweeping ecumenical project that brought together Catholics, Anglicans, and United Church members in ministry in the small and isolated communities of Vancouver Island, St. John's Ecumenical Church, Rumble Beach, worshiped together weekly. The Catholic bishop, the Most Rev. Remi De Roo, observed that what had developed in Port Alice "was a genuine community." He therefore offered them the option of creating a common Eucharistic liturgy based on Eucharistic Prayer n. 2 of the Roman Catholic mass (sometimes called the "Prayer of Hipploytus"). "It is very ancient; it predates the splits in the church catholic, and it was felt that this would be very convenient since it raised no problems theologically. It is also very short, and simple."[23] Thus, in the early 1970s, even before the creation of the Lima Liturgy—the ecumenical Eucharistic service prepared by the World Council of Churches in 1982—the "Port Alice Liturgy for Ecumenical Service" was born, and approved by the Anglican and Roman Catholic bishops and the United Church Presbytery. Three clergy members (one of each denomination) celebrated at the table together. At the time of the Eucharistic prayer, all three said the words together and blessed their own elements. Communicants received the elements according to their respective rites. A form of this liturgy continues to be celebrated periodically in the shared church building at Port Alice.[24]

22. "Since Eucharistic con-celebration is a visible manifestation of full communion in faith, worship, and community life of the Catholic Church, expressed by ministers of that Church, it is not permitted to con-celebrate the Eucharist with ministers of other churches or ecclesial communities." Pontifical Council, par. 104(e).

23. de Roo, interview.

24. Robert Fyles, St. Columba's Anglican United Church, Port Hardy, BC, provided updated information on the Port Alice ministry.

CONFIRMATION AND OTHER CELEBRATIONS

Sunday, May 15, 2011, dawned long anticipated by many of the faithful of St. Peter's Ecumenical Church, in Slave Lake, Alberta. It was Pentecost, and it was confirmation day—the culmination of three years of preparation for a group of Anglican, Lutheran, and United Church of Canada young people. The journey to this day had been rich with learning. Leigh Sinclair described her preparation for conducting confirmation classes in an Anglican/Lutheran/United Church ministry:

> Confirmation . . . is viewed completely differently by our three judicatories: one wants three years of once-a-week sessions; one wants one year of every other week sessions, and one (my home denomination) hopes that you might get six hours under your belt. One wants proper answers to the questions; one wants you to know what to do; and one wants you to know that you can ask any question, that you are empowered to ask questions. Those are three wholly different curricula.[25]

After years of preparation, next came the question of the liturgy:

> I asked each denomination . . . for information and assistance. For the confirmation day, we used the *Book of Alternative Services* liturgy—very close to the Lutheran. The only thing I felt needed to be added was the United Church "New Creed," and I was concerned that there was not enough about justice in the questions, to reflect United Church commitments. So, I drafted a liturgy, and the Anglican bishop tweaked it a little. He came, we co-led the service, and he preached and conducted communion. We both laid hands on everyone. They all took the same vows. It was very powerful.[26]

By two o'clock that Pentecost Sunday afternoon, the town of Slave Lake was on fire, and the entire population was fleeing for their lives down a highway that had flames licking it from both sides. The fire spared the new church, not yet consecrated, but many parishioners lost their homes and everything in them. Others suffered partial damage and several weeks of evacuation. Yet, months later, those who had been part of the confirmation celebration still spoke with awe about the beauty of that liturgy.

Some of the particularly grace-filled moments in multi-denominational ministries occur at confirmation or other rites that demand a special level

25. St. Peter's Ecumenical Church, Sinclair, interview.
26. St. Peter's Ecumenical Church, Sinclair, interview.

of ecumenical awareness and good will. Confirmation, a rite in flux in many Protestant churches, can be a time of consternation for shared ministries. Persons who may have spent their entire lives worshiping as one in a shared ministry must separate themselves into denominational groups. We discuss that membership question further in chapter 11. In the context of worship, however, confirmation also presents an opportunity to demonstrate the "unity in diversity" that is a hallmark of shared ministry. Any opportunity to invite judicatory participation reminds both the parish and the wider church of the special experiment these congregations have undertaken. When the Windermere Valley Shared Ministry (British Columbia) marked its fiftieth anniversary, for example, the Primate of the Anglican Church of Canada, the Most Rev. Fred Hiltz, and the Moderator of the United Church of Canada, the Right Rev. Jordan Cantwell, participated in the Eucharistic celebration.

Denomination-specific liturgies can also present a different kind of ecumenical witness—one tradition observing, respecting, and celebrating with another. It might be as simple as commissioning a member to a denominational office or mission during the Sunday service, or as dramatic as the immersion of Disciples of Christ baptismal candidates in a summer service at a local camp. In these circumstances, shared ministries get the opportunity to model "diversity in unity." We do not do this thing completely in unison, they suggest, but we still do it in solidarity with one another.

"BEING A GIFT TO THE WORLD"

As the participation of traditions less typically associated with shared ministries increases, the opportunity to expand liturgical imaginations also grows. How might spontaneous testimony and regular foot washing change the shape of multi-denominational worship? Surely, they will weave their way into the liturgical life of ecumenical congregations in the same way so many other disparate traditions have done—through a combination of listening, learning, rotating, blending, observing and celebrating. At its fiftieth-anniversary celebration, the people of the Windermere Valley Shared Ministry prayed together, "God of peace, we give thanks as we celebrate . . . the journey that started so many years ago—so many dreams ago. . . . May we be faithful in heeding the Holy Spirit, proclaiming the good news of Jesus, and being a gift to our world."

That is surely the goal of shared congregations at worship: to honor the dreams of those who brought them together by sharing prayer, and then through proclamation and action, being a gift to the world.

8

The Gift(?) of Governance

FOR LOVE, OR FOR MONEY?

On October 31, 1769, forty-seven men gathered at Peaked Mountain, Virginia, and signed their names (or their x's) to a document that began: "In the name of the Triune God and with the consent of the whole congregation, we have commenced to build a new house of God, and it is, by the help of God, so far finished that all the world may see it. We have established it as a union church, in the use of which the Lutherans and their descendants as well as the Reformed and their descendants shall have equal share."[1]

This may be the oldest existing interchurch congregational agreement in North America, representing one of those historic shared parishes described in chapter 5. Written in German, the brief text outlined the parameters of the sharing arrangement. The signatories committed themselves to repair of the church and schoolhouse, and to the salaries of the minister and schoolmaster. Should one of them fail to do so—"which we would not suppose a Christian would do"—that person's membership of the congregation would cease, and he and his family would have to pay, per event, for every baptism, confirmation, burial, and even for participation in Holy Communion.

This was, for the Lutheran and Reformed Christians of Peaked Mountain, a hard-nosed but necessary document. Without this formal agreement, the buildings could go untended, the teacher and minister unpaid. It testifies to a fact persisting nearly 250 years later: interchurch congregations generate paperwork. Because they cross boundaries, and because each one is unique

1. Agreement Between the Reformed and Lutheran Congregations in Peaked Mountain Church.

in its time and place, each multi-denominational congregation[2] must develop its own plans and strategies for shared life. Each interchurch ministry's constitutional document represents the will to create an ecumenical ministry, the patience to shape it, and the permission to proceed.

Over centuries to recent decades, the structures of governance of multi-denominational ministries, and the documents used to describe and prescribe them, have become increasingly complex. In 1978, St. Mark's Churchill Falls, an Anglican-United Church congregation in central Labrador, could get by with a seven-point memorandum. Just over one page in length, it replaced an even briefer memorandum of 1968. It covered the structure of the governing board; the appointment, tenure and responsibilities of the minister/ priest; and the congregation's financial responsibilities.[3] Nearly forty years later, the constitution of Spirit of Grace, a partnership between Our Redeemer Evangelical Lutheran and Asbury United Methodist in Oregon, passed on its ninth draft, comprised nineteen chapters, plus Bylaws.[4] In the United States and Canada until the early 2000s, the governance documents tend to be called "constitutions"; in Canada and in some United States cases, the more recent term is "covenant." Where there is a constitution or covenant as well as by-laws, what goes into each varies from agreement to agreement. Some confine the most judicial elements of their agreement to the constitution (their legal constitution and terms of dissolution), while others include all but the most mutable elements in the constitution.

These agreements give us a glimpse into the conversations and negotiations out of which multi-denominational communities emerge. Just as we can picture a group of eighteenth-century German-speaking farmers in colonial Virginia gathered on their new wooden pews, calculating the cost of their ministry enterprise, we can imagine "the meetings, the many meetings" that went into producing the ecumenical ministry covenant of two historic uptown churches, Presbyterian and United, in Toronto in 2006.[5] Governance documents also remind us of the complex challenge that lies at the heart of the formation of most interchurch congregations: the intersection of love and money. While a few multi-denominational parishes have formed mainly out of desire to model Christian love and unity, most have experienced some

---

2. This chapter uses the singular "congregation" throughout—recognizing that some multi-denominational ministries are multiple congregations gathered into one parish.

3. Memorandum of Agreement, Diocese of Eastern Newfoundland and Labrador and Newfoundland Conference.

4. Constitution and By-Laws for Asbury Our Redeemer Partnership.

5. Deer Park and Calvin, Goodyear, interview.

practical necessity that led them to an ecumenical conversation with their neighbors.[6]

The need to create elaborate governance agreements highlights the material aspects of an interchurch ministry. With their focus on finance, property, and salaries, these constitutions can appear to put law before gospel, money before love. They are ecclesiastical "pre-nups," and they bear some of the stigma and suspicion such legal processes can evoke. Surely, if these Christians care for one another and the church, they do not need to spell out the details before they sign on, do they? Are they just in this to save a few dollars? Further, the process of hammering out the agreement can be intimidating to those exploring interchurch congregational partnerships. Where to begin? What to include? If it takes so much effort, is it worth it?

Indeed, it *is* worth the effort, say those who labor to bring about these agreements. A participant in the formation of an Anglican/United Church parish on the Canadian prairies in the late 1960s described the perseverance required:

> I recall one bogging-down period when the greatest desire seemed to be to forget the whole thing: let each family go east, west, south, wherever, to the church of their choice in other communities and simply close the Evesham building. An elderly gentleman at a particularly crucial meeting . . . asked to lead the opening devotions. He read from Deuteronomy 30. I recall his very short meditation, dramatically emphasized by an unexpected knuckle thumping on the table: "Today I am giving you a choice between life and death; choose life, love the Lord your God, and be faithful." That knuckle thump, the silence that followed, is still a vivid memory. . . . We went back to the table with renewed determination.[7]

While the Peaked Mountain agreement of 1769 only hinted at the Christian commitment involved in creating their Union Church, contemporary multi-denominational constitutions work carefully through practical and spiritual matters. More accurately, they recognize that woven into the material fabric of sharing the building and the pastor's salary is the sharing of Christian life in its many forms: faith, worship, education, leadership, pastoral care. Discussing and setting parameters for life together is a theological act, and the formal agreement is its faithful testimony.

There is, however, the question of the limits of such work. At a congregational meeting of two churches working on the possibility of becoming an

6. Ecumenical Shared Ministries Survey, Canada, as described above, p. 8.

7. Susan Conly, "With Renewed Determination: Unity-Meridian Pastoral Charge," in Barker, *Lively Option*, 3.

interchurch ministry, a lay member asked, "How much agreement do we need? How many things do we need to iron out before we can sign the covenant and get on with it?"[8] It is a good question. Too little consultation and the sharing arrangement can founder when assumptions and expectations differ. Yet in Christian community, there must be room for the Spirit to surprise and challenge. We cannot plan for every contingency, nor satisfy every lingering uncertainty. So how much is enough? This can be a point of contention between congregations and their judicatories, usually with judicatories demanding more detail and specificity than the congregation believes necessary in order to "sign and get on with it." Each multi-denominational congregation and its judicatories will ultimately discern and negotiate the balance for themselves.

This chapter explores ways that shared ministry partners navigate through the planning and governance questions for their ministries. We look at the processes and elements that go into the production of constitutions or covenants, including the types of governance structures that congregations employ, and the ways they handle finances. Then we learn how shared ministry clergy have learned to cope—and thrive—as they assist congregations in meeting the administrative demands of multiple denominations. In all of this, we see love and money—in their many manifestations—as inseparable aspects of shared Christian life, and that governance—at its best—is a gift that helps Christians engage in their mission with integrity.

FROM DREAM TO REALITY: SHAPING A FORMAL INTERCHURCH MINISTRY AGREEMENT

"Where do we start?" Every interchurch partnership begins in a different place. It usually involves some combination of friendship, curiosity, and needs assessment among parishioners, clergy, and judicatory leaders. Casual conversations, suggestions by leaders, experiments with combined liturgies and other events, and informal meetings begin the process. Once begun, if there is genuine interest in pursuing the possibilities, each partnership will take its own path to a formal agreement. However, there are also steps that, if followed, make the journey less tortuous.

Perhaps the most insistent advice is, as a set of United Church of Canada guidelines puts it, "Always begin by contacting your presbytery." That is, get the judicatories involved right away, if they have not been part of the initial conversation. In the best circumstances, these people will have not only the information and expertise to guide the process, but also the pastoral skills

---

8. Author's experience, November 2015.

to hearten the participants. If the partners are in a full communion or other ecumenical covenant, it is likely there are guidelines specific to that covenant. Denominations also have their own policies or canons, and judicatories can make the partners aware of these. There will be legal matters at stake. Some multi-denominational congregations are able to continue under a previous not-for-profit designation, while others will seek a new designation. Many interchurch congregations report that the judicatories were helpful and encouraging. Even when they are less than enthusiastic sharing information is crucial. No church leader wants to be taken by surprise.

There will be meetings. Of course, there will be meetings. They are crucial not only to the actual agreement, but also to the building of fellowship and trust. Moreover, like the judicatories, the congregants of potential multi-denominational unions need to be kept informed with regular updates. One congregation kept binders of minutes by each of the sanctuary doors to keep the process accessible and transparent.[9] In the course of these discussions, the elements of a formal agreement will emerge. While the order may vary, the following issues need to be addressed and most will appear in some form in the formal agreement.

Statement of Mission

Names what those covenanting together believe they are called to be and do. Some are brief:

> Believing there is one God, revealed in Jesus Christ and made real to us each day through the Holy Spirit, our mission is to provide a sharing, caring, worshipping community, based on Christian ministry, where all are welcome."[10]

Other mission statements may be several paragraphs long and may highlight their ecumenical nature as part of their statement:

> The special purpose of the United Christian Parish is to exemplify in tangible ways the prayer of Jesus "that they may all be one" (John 17:20).[11]

> We, the people of the Church of the Holy Apostles, united by faith in Jesus Christ . . . seeking to deepen our own faith lives and thus

9. Deer Lake and Calvin, Goodyear, interview.

10. Covenant, Trinity Lutheran Church of Spiritwood and Bissell Memorial Church of Spiritwood, 1.

11. Constitution, United Christian Parish of Reston, 4.

helping to heal the wounds which separate Christians from one another . . . do ordain and establish this constitution.[12]

A very few go into detail about matters of faith. The constitution of Asbury Our Redeemer Partnership interchurch parish includes four pages of text that feature an eighteen-point Confession of Faith, a six-point statement on the Nature of the Church, and a six-part Statement of Purpose, drawn in part from a bilateral faith statement of their two participating denominations.[13]

Definition

Outlines the congregation's formal denominational partners, and how the members retain membership in the congregation and in their own denominations.

Relationship to Participating Denominations

Spells out the "definition" more fully. This may include affirming the congregation's commitments to the service and work of the denominations, and their promise to provide reports to fulfill other denominational responsibilities. It may specify the protocols (constitution, manual, discipline) to which the partners are responsible. Some agreements spell out the potential situation of "conflicting mandatory provisions"—times when the sponsoring denominations differ in their demands of members. In these cases, the sponsoring judicatories need to resolve the problem. However, some interchurch congregations have prior permission of their judicatories to privilege their own constitutions if they stand in conflict with one or more judicatory constitutions.[14]

Membership

Describes how persons live out their congregational and their denominational membership. In multi-denominational ministry, membership is not straightforward. (See chapter 11 on multiple religious belonging.) This part of an agreement seeks to clarify that persons are members of the shared congregation and of a specific denomination:

12. Constitution, Church of the Holy Apostles, Richmond, Virginia, 1.

13. Constitution and By-Laws for Asbury, chapters 2–4.

14. See, for example, Constitution and Bylaws for Asbury Partnership, ch. 6, C6.05–C6.06.

> The membership of Sunriver Christian Fellowship . . . is composed of Christians who have publicly expressed a desire to join and participate fully in the life of the Congregation. Individuals who are or become members of the Sponsoring Congregations in accordance with their traditions are also members.[15]

Sometimes, the agreement spells out the ecumenical vision implied in congregational membership:

> Looking ahead in a spirit of ecumenism toward sharing the uniqueness of our Christian heritage, committed to a total ministry of stewardship, all members shall strive to attain fuller unity in Jesus Christ, and to become a Church organically united.[16]

The membership section of an agreement also explains how those baptized in, or received into, the congregation determine their denominational membership. There may also be a clause about how the parochial records are to be maintained; on these matters, the sponsoring denominations may have already set guidelines.

Ministry

Explains the appointment of the (paid) pastoral leaders of the congregation. This section specifies the denominational affiliation required and the process for appointment. It may also describe the pastor's relationship to the participating denominations and the role of the pastor on the congregation's governing body. It can further outline the responsibilities of the ministry staff, the process to be followed in case of conflict, and the termination policy, which may be at the behest of the pastor's judicatory person or body. Historically, multi-denominational ministries have attempted to "rotate" clergy between or among the participating denominations. In practice, many congregations prefer the pastor who is the "best fit," recognizing that a good multi-denominational pastor will be sensitive to denominational needs regardless of his or her own affiliation.

Governance Structure

Outlines the decision-making structure of the shared ministry. Many structures are possible. Some interchurch congregations act as an umbrella that

15. By-Laws of Sunriver Christian Fellowship, Inc., Section 4.01, 2.
16. Constitution of Church of the Holy Apostles, Article I, Section 1.

overarches two or more continuing congregations that have chosen to worship and work together. The more common pattern is to merge the existing participating congregations into a new entity. Regardless of how they come together, interchurch ministries need to address two issues that are specific to their ecumenical sharing: how to allow for denomination-specific decision-making, and how to ensure the unified governance body honors both the union and the distinctiveness of the partnership.

Denomination-Specific Governance

The congregation will need a mechanism for fulfilling its responsibilities to the sponsoring denominations, from electing members to regional bodies to receiving and sharing denominational information. In a small congregation, this might amount to holding denomination-specific caucus meetings at least once a year to make appointments and nominations and to review denominational requests. At the other end of the spectrum, the parish board of the four-denomination United Christian Parish of Reston, Virginia includes an ecumenical council, which takes responsibility for "establishing, maintaining, and enhancing communications and interactions with our affiliated denominations and the interfaith community in the Reston area." It consists of four denominational liaison persons (who are also Board members) and one member of the ministerial team.[17] The Church of the Holy Apostles includes a similar ecumenical council as part of its vestry council.[18]

Unified Governance

This body can bear any of a variety of names: joint church council, parish board, board of governors, managing board, vestry council, or parish leadership team, to name a few. It consists of the ministry personnel and elected lay members. In most congregations, there are also standing committees that report to this governing body. Unified governance also occurs through annual congregational meetings. Some congregations specify minimum quotas of membership from each of their sponsoring denominations on their governing body and/or committees; many do not. Two additional features also make this governance unique to multi-denominational ministries: how they deal with those who are fully members of the congregation, but *not* of one of the

17. United Christian Parish Constitution, IV, Section D.1, 8–9. See also their By-Laws, IV. Section A, 22.

18. Constitution of Holy Apostles, Bylaws, third amendment (2012).

sponsoring denominations, and how they incorporate, if at all, the particular oversight charisms of their participating traditions. A brief review follows.

The "Others"

The presence and active participation of Christians who belong to denominations other than those who have signed onto the formal agreement is common across multi-denominational ministries. Some congregations accept them as full members of the congregation, eligible for board membership. Some specify that up to a certain portion of the board can consist of non-sponsoring church members. At least one, the three-denomination St. Peter's Ecumenical Church of Slave Lake, Alberta, divides its board four ways, with equal representation from each of its three sponsoring denominations and from the category they called "other."[19]

Participating Traditions

Congregations may wish to uphold in their new ministry elements embedded deeply within their Christian denominational traditions. Thus, a congregation with Anglican/Episcopalian sponsorship may designate one or more lay positions on its board as wardens, with specific tasks of leadership and assistance to the clergy.[20] Those with Presbyterian and Christian Church (Disciples of Christ) sponsorship may ordain or install lay elders and deacons.

In the end, the governance section(s) of a formal interchurch congregational agreement will appear not unlike any single-denomination congregational constitution. It will include—in various degrees of elaboration suitable to the context—election procedures; names, functions, and membership of committees or ministry teams; the status of denominational organizations (such as local expressions of denominational women's groups); and processes for congregational meetings.

Worship Life

Describes how the liturgical life of the interchurch ministry will unfold. Despite the centrality of worship practices to these congregations, few of them spell out the details of worship life in their formal agreements. Denominational

---

19. St. Peter's Ecumenical Church, Procyshyn, interview.
20. See, for example, Bylaws of Spirit of Grace, Sylvan Lake, VII.B, 7.

guidelines tend not to demand that worship practices find their way into the constitution. Where they do appear, they cover such things as the worship schedule, the rotation of worship rites, and the role of visiting worship leaders.[21]

Property/Assets

Covers the sometimes-complex questions of the ownership and management of buildings and other material assets. In certain cases, the congregation will dispose of one building, in order to use its funds to maintain the other, common building. The shared building is held jointly in the names of both (or all) participating denominations. Partners in Worship, a Lutheran (ELCIC) and United Church of Canada congregation in rural Saskatchewan, decided to use the United Church, and to move the Lutheran church hall, joining it to the United Church. When the two buildings were put together, their rooflines matched perfectly. The congregation took this as a providential sign their new partnership was meant to be.[22] The Episcopal-Lutheran (ELCA) Sunriver Christian Fellowship in Oregon turned its agreement on property matters into a theological testimony:

> Recognizing the unity and uniqueness of SCF, each constituency and each Judicatory subordinates its beneficial interest in the real property and/or financial assets of SCF to the common interest and benefit of the SCF Congregation.[23]

Finances

Determines the apportionment of funds to the congregation's various ministries and denominational obligations. This may be the sort of nightmare that makes people unwilling to take on the role of the church treasurer. However, there are templates to assist a multi-denominational ministry in finding the best plan for its stewardship. Some interchurch congregations do not form a new legal entity. They operate financially as two (or more) congregations sharing some ministry and contributing to it from their separate funds. More often, the multi-denominational congregation is a new legal being. In these cases,

21. Memorandum of Understanding, Cedarcroft, 2, devotes considerable attention to worship rites, times, and special liturgies.

22. Ratzlaff, Wiig, Pek, and McGowan, *God's Reconciling Grace*, 79.

23. Covenant Agreement and By-Laws, Sunriver.

there are three "pots" of money at stake: donations for congregational purposes (including the congregation's outreach), denominational apportionments, and denominational mission funds. Here are ways to manage each.

Donations for Congregational Purposes

As with a single-denomination ministry, these are collected from donor pledges, weekly offerings, and fund-raising efforts, to be disbursed under the control of the governing board, according to any directives of the participating denominations. For example, a denomination may specify that the pastor's salary will be paid first from any local funds.

Denominational Apportionments

Many denominations assess annual dues to each congregational ministry, based on membership. The determination of the precise formula for an interchurch congregation requires the consent and cooperation of the sponsoring denominations. It should not encumber the congregation with more "dues" than a single-denomination ministry would bear. Most opt for a policy like that developed by the national church council of the ELCA: such per capita assessments are "paid to each ecclesiastical entity of jurisdiction based on the total active membership" of the congregation, "equally divided among the churches involved."[24] If one of the sponsoring denominations does not assess annual dues, the congregation can allot an amount equal to their share of the apportionment to that denomination's mission fund or other denominational project.

Denominational Mission Funds

Each sponsoring denomination invites its members to participate financially in its wider mission. Interchurch congregations need to allow givers to designate donations to the mission fund of their choice, but also may budget, through their governing boards, for particular denominational projects. A church treasurer for a three-denomination interchurch ministry noted that while the church envelope has options for all three denominational mission

---

24. Evangelical Lutheran Church in America, "Documents of Governance and Policy," 4, 5–6.

funds, many donors will tick all three boxes, or just write "mission" on the donation.[25]

Withdrawal/Termination Clause

Describes how one denominational partner might withdraw from the inter-church congregation, and what happens if the entire congregation ceases to exist. Unhappy as it may be to consider, such a clause may assuage the fears of the skeptical, and assure anxious judicatories. The clause usually clarifies ownership of property, and may also name the minimum notice required for withdrawal. At least one multi-denominational ministry is not quite ready to accept that such pecuniary issues are in keeping with Christian faithfulness. Sunriver Christian Fellowship makes the following statement regarding the withdrawal of support by one denomination or sponsoring congregation:

> Considering the presently unknown facts and circumstances that would attend such events . . . no provision is made for such events or occurrences. The parties to this covenant Agreement pledge their intent to negotiate in good faith, based on the circumstances then existing, to reach a result that is equitable and acceptable to all parties in the event some such development occurs.[26]

GOVERNANCE ADMINISTRATION: CRAZY-MAKING, OR TOOL OF UNITY?

A facilitator asked a gathering of clergy serving interchurch congregations: "What is your biggest frustration in ecumenical shared ministry?" Most of them replied, "The forms! The endless forms! Doing every administrative task in duplicate or triplicate, but slightly differently for each. Can't the churches get their act together and create a common form for us?"[27] Their plea did not go unheeded; the four main denominations involved in Canadian interchurch ministries developed a "joint statistical form," which could be completed once and submitted to all the sponsoring judicatories.

It was a good start, but clergy involved in ecumenical shared ministries still struggle with the multiple expectations of their sponsoring denominations.

---

25. St. Peter's Ecumenical Church, Procyshyn, interview.

26. Covenant Agreement and By-Laws, Sunriver, 3.

27. Ecumenical Shared Ministries Conference, Winnipeg, Manitoba (January 1993). Author's experience.

"Because we are three denominations, we tend to be hard on our ministers," said Janice Nowochin.[28] Those who thrive in these parishes find ways to take charge of the expectations before becoming overwhelmed. These clergy make choices, based on careful reasoning, about which opportunities and requests they will fulfill. They usually make their own denomination's demands upon them a first priority, while trying to accommodate a few of the others. For some clergy, however, this kind of ministry represents an opportunity to live the ecumenical life more deeply. As the Rev. Ray Cuthbert of Broadway Disciples United Church, Winnipeg, described it:

> I go to [the United Church of Canada] Presbytery every month. I have been on its Presbytery executive, and the [United Church] Conference Planning Committee. I am not any longer just a Disciples minister. If I am going to do ministry, part of my goal is to model what I expect of others. I have to be invested, if I expect my people to be invested. . . . The wider church work is a lot of time and a lot of engagement. But if you don't do it, you have a harder time laying claim to the [ecumenical] vision.[29]

Multi-denominational ministry pastors also affirm that good administrative assistance, even in a small congregation, can make a huge difference.

> If your church does not have a secretary you can trust, you need to get one! I open three times the mail, and I need to know where it all goes.[30]

> I would highly recommend her [the parish administrator] to God, if God needs an administrator. She is competent, she is willing, she is calm. She has been an incredible source of strength. That, to me, has helped to make this work. There is continuity.[31]

Administrative demands can also be a source of ecumenical engagement and education. Some multi-denominational clergy use it as an opportunity for lay leaders to enter into an ecumenical dialogue. After reviewing the educational materials circulated by their participating denominations, they can ask, "What are the theological similarities and differences in their approaches and underlying assumptions about Christian life and learning?" This can lead to reflection on which denomination's mission goal or project to focus on this year, and why. The structures of governance can also be a learning tool: What

28. St. Peter's Ecumenical, Nowochin, interview.

29. Broadway Disciples United, Cuthbert, interview.

30. St. Peter's Ecumenical, Sinclair, interview.

31. Deer Park and Calvin, Goodyear, interview.

does a warden do? Why do Anglicans have them? How is it possible that a congregation can "ordain" a lay leader? Wherever did the Reformed Church get that idea?

Not least, the congregation's formal constitutional agreement reminds the members, lovingly, of its own mission—one that reaches, however modestly, beyond personal satisfaction to a deeper share in the life of the gospel, with one another, with the rest of the church, and with the world. In that spirit, we may, after all the endless meetings, after all the many words and phrases have been debated and refined and the dotted line has been signed, after all that, we may see governance as indeed a gift to ecumenical ministry.

9

Maintaining Good Judicatory Relations

AMONG THE MANY WATERS multi-denominational congregations bridge is polity. It can be calm, a steady stream of mutual benign neglect or, at other times, a raging torrent of misunderstanding and resentment. How do these congregations respond or contribute to such states of affairs? How do two bishops relate to the same parish? Or, how do leaders relate who have entirely different titles and functions, such as executive presbyters, presidents, or bishops? How do dioceses, presbyteries, and congregational associations interact? What does the ministry of these ecumenical congregations contribute to the ongoing dialogue about the nature of individual and corporate oversight? Who is the boss? To begin answering these questions, we briefly review three major forms of polity (each with dozens of variations, depending upon the tradition), moving on to consider some multi-denominational congregations "in action" where polity is concerned, especially the calling or appointment of clergy.

Thirty-one clergy serving multi-denominational congregations in the United States were asked in a survey about relationships with their judicatories. While they reported a variety of patterns, slightly over half habitually attend (with or without lay delegates) all the judicatory gatherings to which their local church relates.

Respondents were also asked about five challenging factors in a shared ministry: finances, conflicts in worship and theology, congregational discomfort with the arrangement, future planning, and lack of judicatory support. Only two of the thirty-one cited lack of judicatory support as their greatest concern, although some gave it a high priority. Based on these respondents, we can surmise lack of understanding by a judicatory is only a moderate concern. When asked about the reasons for forming their multi-denominational congregation, three of the thirty-one said encouragement by related judicatories was very important, seven said it was somewhat or not important, and five said their judicatories' support was "not applicable" in the decision.

In reply to a third, related question in the survey—"Does the judicatory to which you relate value the multi-denominational ministry?"—seven respondents suggested their judicatories "prized their congregation as a model of Christian unity"; nine saw it primarily as a means for financial convenience; seven thought their judicatories would like to foster more such congregations in their regions, and six thought their judicatories failed to understand or appreciate ecumenical congregations. Almost as many judicatories are puzzled by as value the multi-denominational congregations in their purview, and a sizable portion see them as financially expedient arrangements.

In Canada, as we have seen, judicatories historically have played a significant role either in initiating or in terminating ecumenical shared ministries. In the past decade, the four churches most involved in shared ministries have cooperated to produce a national Ecumenical Shared Ministry handbook with guidelines for judicatories, clergy, and congregations. Shared ministry congregations continue to express mixed views of their judicatory relationships. On one hand, in our Canadian survey, over sixty percent of respondents said the judicatories had encouraged the formation of the shared ministry. Forty-five percent of respondents stated that support and encouragement from the judicatory leadership of the participating denominations was "very important," another forty-five percent said it was "somewhat important" for the effective functioning of their shared ministry parish. On the other hand, lack of judicatory support and assistance ranked second (after lack of financial resources) as one of the most vexing aspects of the sharing experience. While respondents reported their relationships with judicatories were either good or not "a problem," there was an undercurrent of frustration. One respondent commented:

> Our challenge is not really with a lack of judicatory support; they are supportive of the arrangement, but not so supportive that they will negotiate with each other so our congregation could make one set of administrative reports which are shared between the two. Both require their own documentation, on their own timetables.

It takes a great deal of time, which is at a premium since we also share one clergy person with two other congregations of one of the two denominations in our arrangement.[1]

ONE CHURCH: MANY KINDS OF OVERSIGHT

Traditions in which oversight is at least partially centralized in an individual are called episcopal, from the Greek for "overseer," usually translated "bishop." Eastern Orthodox, Roman Catholic, Anglican/Episcopal, Moravian, most Lutheran, Methodist, and some Pentecostal traditions have bishops who oversee mission and ministry in a given geographical locale, variably called a diocese, province, synod, or conference, depending on the denomination. In some cases, such as Orthodoxy and Catholicism, bishops carry great authority in decision-making, clergy appointment, and setting the tone for their dioceses through annual visitations to their parishes. This is also true to some extent among world Anglican bishops, who, with their Orthodox and Catholic colleagues, administer confirmation. Bishops in all three of these traditions accept (or reject) candidates for ordination, guiding them through educational requirements and other preparations.

Variations come into play. For instance, American Episcopal bishops facilitate a clergy call process and do not appoint priests to parishes, much as in presbyterian and congregationalist polities. Canadian Anglican bishops appoint clergy to parishes, with congregational input. Lutheran and United Methodist bishops typically do not visit their local congregations annually nor administer confirmation, but preside at yearly synod or conference assemblies and act as *pastor pastorum* (pastor to the pastors), and ultimately, to the whole flock in their charge. United Methodist bishops have unilateral authority in the appointive process, with pastors moved about in the annual conference, if no longer on a four-year cycle, at least when needs dictate the move of a pastor with certain abilities to a church that could benefit. Judicatories served by bishops may feature varying degrees of lay leadership, and the presence of myriads of committees populated by clergy and lay incumbents who administer finances, approve ordinands, and otherwise share in judicatory governance, somewhat relativizing a bishop's authority.

Some episcopally-governed churches place great value on the doctrine of apostolic succession, a belief that bishops are set apart by the laying on of hands in a chain of hands going back to the apostles. Bishops outside such

---

1. Respondent, Canadian ESM survey (see p. 8).

a chain are deemed irregular, at best, and the churches they serve, however faithful in other respects, are fundamentally "defective" or lacking an essential feature.[2] This has been a major ecumenical hurdle, which, while practically nonexistent now among episcopal Protestant churches, persists between them and their Catholic and Orthodox counterparts.

Congregationalist polity claims the authority of antiquity—the New Testament church—as does episcopal. Here, local congregations exercise complete authority over their mission and ministry, and voluntarily join wider judicatories, for instance, a Baptist association, to work together with other area congregations on common interests, such as the support of missionaries or local outreach projects. A congregational church calls and dismisses its own clergy, owns its property outright, and sets other standards for itself, including theological. If asked "What about bishops mentioned in I Timothy 3?" a congregationalist might note that "overseer" in the early church meant something like a "senior pastor" in a local church who was accompanied by a staff of elders—associate pastors in effect—and aided by deacons, servant ministers who saw to the needs of widows, orphans, and the poor. Hence, congregationalists have claimed the historic New Testament offices of ministry for the local church, removing them from higher echelons of geographical authority.

Denominations in the Reformed/Presbyterian family are defined by a distinctive polity in which bishops are conspicuously absent, but congregations are not independent. This absence goes back to reformers such as John Calvin and John Knox, who rejected the authority exercised by diocesan bishops as an illegitimate development that created a monarchy within the church, whereby power was centralized and laity had no share in church life, except, in effect, to "pray, pay, and obey." In place of a monarchical episcopate, Calvin developed a system of four offices based on his New Testament studies, including teaching and ruling elders, pastors, and deacons. This model insured parity between lay and clerical functions (illustrating the priesthood of all believers) and made possible a Reformed representative democracy, where lay and clerical officers in equal numbers represented local churches at regional synods or presbyteries. "Presbyterian" names this distinctive pattern in which groups of elders—lay and clerical—provide checks and balances on one another. To vest authority in one person—one sinner among many—was to invite the worst of human nature into the governance of the church, thought Calvin. His Augustinian anthropology was far too low to entertain the possibility of

2. Cf., Flannery, *Vatican Council II*, "Decree on Ecumenism," par. 22. "The Chicago-Lambeth Quadrilateral" of 1886 listed "The Historic Episcopate, locally adapted in the methods of its administration to the varying needs of the nations and peoples called of God into the unity of His Church" as an essential feature of church unity. See Episcopal Church, *Book of Common Prayer*, 876–78.

a singular human authority! At least councils of elders both ordained and lay could check one another to some extent.

This form came in for challenge wherever episcopal structures dominated, as in the British Isles, where Reformed theology made inroads well enough, though Presbyterian polity was, with some intriguing exceptions, not accepted by the Anglican Church. This was especially true in Scotland, where the Presbyterian Church gained a stronghold but had to contend with an episcopacy beholden to the crown.[3] Bishops were rejected in Reformed circles due to theological, exegetical, and historical reasons.

Presbyterians and Anglicans/Episcopalians lived in social proximity to one another in Canada and the United States where they formed a significant part of the Protestant mainline core, two traditions with a broadly common theological foundation but vastly different polities. On the Anglican side, there historically have been those who have contended for bishops as of the *bene esse* of the church—they are signs, but not guarantors, of good order and sound teaching. There have also been parties within Anglicanism—especially the Anglo-Catholics who grew out of the Oxford Movement of the 1830s and 1840s—who view the episcopate as of the *esse* of the church, and therefore a necessary fixture in all ecumenical proposals. The 1888 Lambeth Quadrilateral called for four non-negotiables in all Anglican ecclesial accords with other communions, namely, the Bible, the historic creeds, baptism and eucharist, and some form of the historic episcopate, i.e., bishops ordained in apostolic succession.[4]

Given all these variations, and with this historical background in mind, are episcopal, congregational, and presbyterian forms of governance incompatible? How do these differing polities affect attempts of a shared ministry to function in basic matters, such as pastoral calls and appointment? We turn to examples of multi-denominational congregations related to differing polities, and suggest how ecumenical congregations can relate positively and with equanimity to their sponsoring judicatories. Since clergy deployment often necessitates close association with their judicatories, we now consider the process followed by Trinity Ecumenical Parish (TEP) in Smith Mountain Lake, Virginia (see chapter 4).

Trinity is a multi-denominational parish comprised of Episcopal, Lutheran, and Presbyterian congregations, each with its own vestry, council, and session, respectively. The parish is united in worship, ministry, and mission, calls pastors from the three traditions, and has an overarching parish council. The three parish governing entities—vestry, council, and session—are the

3. Small, "Ecclesial Identity," 3.

4. *Book of Common Prayer*, 1979, 876–78.

channels for relating to each judicatory with "reports, elections, representation at judicatory assemblies, etc." The parish council and annual business meeting function as overarching bodies handling local affairs, including pastoral calls, property issues, and overall budget. The three judicatories must approve the joining of additional denominations to the parish as well as any other changes to the Covenant Agreement. Matters pertaining to property have also been ratified by the judicatories. The covenant agreement, where these rubrics are contained, insures understanding on all sides. Attention to detail in governance may be a key ingredient in the assertion that "At Trinity, differences are common; conflict is rare."[5]

The church's transition team, by which TEP called a new associate pastor, used a sixty-step transition map, an instructive example of careful planning and interaction with its three judicatories. The church may advertise for a pastor from any of the three traditions and so engages with all three judicatories at once and in accordance with the expectations of each. Call profiles for each denomination, posted on the church's website, outline the detailed "map" of the call process in a way that minimizes misunderstandings between local and regional bodies, including what is supposed to happen next.

Perhaps therein lies the secret of the TEP governing body's careful attention to detail. Nothing is left to chance, and parish and judicatories are fully apprised of each step and attentive to variance in practice. Is too much sometimes left to assumption in multi-denominational congregations that can come back to bite? The assumption that everyone involved "knows" expectations, or that matters will be handled one way and not another can lead to unnecessary conflict and ill will. If one denomination tends to dominate a shared congregation, assuming charge of buildings and programs, it can well follow that this is in imitation of attitudes at the judicatory level.

Another factor in Trinity Ecumenical Parish's self-understanding and its relationship to three judicatories is the Covenant Agreement, ratified in 1991, when the parish was in its infancy. The statement establishes a reciprocal principle among all stakeholders. It explains that Trinity is committed to all three judicatories and expects them "to support our ecumenical venture as the sole expression of each denomination in the Smith Mountain Lake area for the immediate future" (Preamble). Mutual ministry between parish and judicatory is underscored in the document: "The judicatories authorize the Vestry, the Lutheran Council, and the Session to function in those areas of congregational life which pertain uniquely to the three congregations. And in

---

5. Trinity Ecumenical Parish, "Covenant of Agreement," church website.

like fashion, the judicatories authorize the Parish Council to govern all other aspects of the parish's life."[6]

WHO'S THE BOSS?

But not all goes well in every multi-denominational congregation's relationship to its judicatories. If "who's the boss" is in question locally, often it will be questioned regionally. Both congregations and judicatories register complaints. Aggravations among the congregations are judicatories who neglect to recognize and encourage locations of potential ecumenical sharing, or, when they see enthusiasm for such sharing, express over-caution; bureaucratic tangles that inhibit the formation and thriving of multi-denominational ministries; judicatories placing or approving ministry personnel who are inappropriate for the congregation; the granting of only limited pastoral authority to ministry personnel of another denomination; judicatories who constantly express wariness about the potential loss of denominational identity within congregations; and judicatories who terminate shared ministries when conflict emerges, instead of helping them to work it through.

Meanwhile, judicatory leaders note that oversight is often more complex than individual congregations recognize: multipoints, regional boundaries, and other logistical issues must be considered. They contend congregations sometimes want to rush into sharing without taking the time to get to know one another. Further, ministry personnel are hard to find and place in multi-denominational parishes, which are often in geographically "challenging" areas while also requiring persons with ecumenical knowledge and sensitivity. Relating ecumenically adds another burden to an already overstretched judicatory role.

A common perception among some multi-denominational congregations is that judicatories are mostly concerned with their church's procedures not being sullied with those of another. In one congregation uniting two traditions of varying liturgical observance, the bishop of the more liturgical tradition expressed pleasure that his side of the flock was "coming around" to reclaiming their denominational ways in worship, rather than sacrificing them in the name of unity. A judicatory leader expressed exasperation regarding a multi-denominational congregation in his territory that he perceived could not "make up its mind which it wanted to be." Bridging a call and an appointment system, he explained, created friction every time a new minister came by one system or the other, with the party belonging to the opposite

6. Trinity Ecumenical Parish, "Covenant of Agreement," church website.

system balking at having to "relearn" the reasoning for the process every time and finding it objectionable. "It would make mission and ministry easier just to amicably separate." One judicatory administrator admits to being unimpressed with the shared ministry model, arguing that a joint church needs strong lay leadership who understand the polities involved and who do not resent the one(s) who do not represent his or her native tradition. The problem comes with endless arguments over the way one judicatory deploys clerical leadership.

What if ecumenical congregations lean toward one or another polity, proportional to membership; do adherents to the other form end up resentful? At that point, does a judicatory intervene? Does the matter then become one of "rights" for the slighted constituency, thus building more resentment among those seeing the intervention as a heavy hand directing them to "do it our way"? Bad relationships can come from the local to the regional level as well. One church claimed one of their constituent judicatories "barely knew them," and, the judicatory, in turn, claimed that in multiple attempts at communication with the local shared ministry, all were ignored. Plenty can go wrong where a single denomination is involved; even more can go askew where there are two or more. Mission and ministry are stifled by such incidents, and even the earnest believers in the ecumenical vision begin to doubt and look elsewhere for a congregation. One administrator noted that if a joint parish is left with only documents—the disciplines or canon laws of the represented churches and a local covenant document—such literature is insufficient to provide the leadership needed to make the local church function well. The premise of all shared ministry work must come from Jesus, when he says, "love one another!" (John 13:34).

Said Mrs. Sharon Corriveau of Sparwood: "We are fulfilling God's purpose. The problem is with the hierarchy."[7] Are there ways of mitigating this notion locally so that relationships are more productive?

One way that multi-denominational congregations can foster constructive relationships with their governing bodies is to choose the role of educator. They should be intentional about speaking up about the nature of their ministry in wider assemblies where many eyes and ears are present. Why not set up a display at the next regional gathering? Offer to give a presentation or perhaps a workshop on "how to start a new multi-denominational ministry." Have a choir or youth group participate in proceedings. Sponsor resolutions or legislation that magnifies the ecumenical commitments of their denominations. Without this activism, the idea may persist among judicatory leaders and churches that the multi-denominational congregation in their midst is

7. Kootenay Presbytery Minutes, Oct. 17–19, 1976.

"not a normal church," or represents a last-resort survival strategy rather than a sign of the Spirit doing something new.

In some cases, judicatory leaders can do a better job of appreciating the unique opportunities their ecumenical congregations represent, starting with prioritizing ecumenism in their territory wherever possible. "Ecumenical relations are far down my list," admitted one bishop. This attitude cannot persist while expecting the church to expand in the new and exciting ways ecumenism affords. In many cases, where a mission start of one denomination alone might not be viable, an ecumenical ministry would. How many mission developers think of this? What opportunities abound for new church starts in unlikely places using a multi-denominational model? Judicatories already committed to ecumenical life—and there are many—should, like local ecumenical congregations, invite attention to this activity as a way of inspiring their less-ecumenically minded neighbors. In so doing, perhaps the anxious question of "Who's the boss?" will become less pressing under the Spirit's creative guidance.

PART III

Futures

10

Formation for Service in a Multi-Denominational Congregation

CLERGY IN MULTI-DENOMINATIONAL PARISHES tend to love what they do. "I would probably have left ministry many years ago if not for ecumenical shared ministry and would find it difficult, if not impossible, to return to single denomination ministry. One- denominational ministry would feel," one of our survey respondents wrote, "like a step backwards." That same survey showed that one of the main priorities for these congregations is being served by ministry personnel who are excited about ecumenical ministry and willing to help make it work. How do such ministry personnel prepare themselves for these ministries?

In her 2016 book, *Seminary Formation: Recent History, Current Circumstances, New Directions*, Katarina Schuth challenges seminaries to form students "for a wide catholicity." Too often, she laments, "the whole issue of other churches and religions is simply not on their radar screens."[1] The clergy and laity of multi-denominational parishes agreed. Many clergy admitted that they came to this call with little or no experience with the partner denomination. Many had little knowledge of the ecumenical agreements of their own churches. But all had developed a deep commitment to this new form of ministry and expressed their hope that others might come to this endeavor better prepared than they themselves had been. The laity described how hard it had been to hire clergy with an ecumenical heart to serve in these calls and wanted seminarians to consider the potential life-giving and life-changing nature of this ministry.

1. Schuth, *Seminary Formation*, 126–27.

This chapter offers practical preparation guidance to seminarians, clergy, and judicatory leaders who feel called to serve or to help create and support a multi-denominational ministry. What does a seminarian need to include in his/her learning goals in order to gain the knowledge needed? Whether seminarian or experienced pastor, what kinds of formation for ministry does one need? And how might one be open to the transformative work of the Holy Spirit to be shaped into a minister with an ecumenical worldview? How might one become equipped to offer a faithful response to Jesus' call to this kind of ministry? This preparation engages every level of church: laity, clergy, judicatory heads, and theologians.

Seminaries and divinity schools will differ in their approaches. Formation for ecumenical ministry can happen in a variety of educational contexts through a range of pedagogical approaches. The key characteristic is a holistic and intentional learning experience, not just a random encounter with denominational diversity. Formation is indeed about mastering a body of material, but it requires experiential, spiritual, theological, and pastoral dimensions as well.

Veteran ecumenical leader Michael Kinnamon describes twelve qualities that he considers essential in an ecumenical leader:

1   Compelling and infectious vision of God's intended wholeness;

2   Capacity for empathy;

3   Willingness to tolerate anxiety when faced with the unfamiliar;

4. Appreciation for the ecumenical movement and its various "streams";

5. Humility to put themselves in the background;

6. Courage to hold the churches accountable for the commitments they make to one another;

7. Ability to live with disagreement;

8. Appreciation for the church being local and global;

9. Recognition that ecumenical leaders exercise only "charismatic" authority;

10. Conviction that this work is ministry;

11. Spiritual depth needed to face loneliness and frustration; and

12. Unshakable hope in God's future.[2]

2. Kinnamon, *Can a Renewal Movement Be Renewed?*, 137–45.

Our research corroborates Kinnamon's list. In our parish interviews for this book, a researcher asked the clergy and laity at each shared ministry parish for their wisdom and advice for seminarians who will become the clergy for the next generation of ecumenical shared ministry parishes. Their responses were varied and insightful. From these data, we assert that seven distinctive student-learning outcomes are necessary for the formation of seminarians and clergy for effective ministry in multi-denominational parishes. While not all of these are unique to ecumenical shared ministries, they are, nevertheless, critically important characteristics and skills for those serving in these ministries.

DEVELOPING AN ECUMENICAL HEART AND MIND-SET

Effective ministry in a multi-denominational parish takes a deep commitment to Jesus' prayer for Christian unity as God's call upon one's life. Students preparing for this vocation need a love for the church catholic and a dedicated interest in serving God's people in a range of expressions of faith. The call of Jesus to make visible the unity that Christ shares with the Father and the Holy Spirit is their primary motivation for ministry.

The Roman Catholic deacon serving Holy Apostles Episcopal-Roman Catholic parish in Virginia Beach paid tribute to the ecumenical passion of his Episcopal priest counterpart.

> I think one of the reasons why this community has done well through the trials over the last couple of years is because of the commitment of Mike [Ferguson] who has been willing to see it through because of his commitment to the community and the ecumenism. A lesser pastor would have just folded up his tent and moved out. I think that you have to be committed to ecumenism, you have to understand that collaboration is going to be important, and that it is going to be a lot more work than the other. If what you see is Christian unity as your goal, you are going to see the rewards to support the extra effort. If, on the other hand, you are just trying to get by, then you are going to say, "This is too hard."[3]

Seminaries play a major role in the denominational branding problem discussed in chapter 12. They focus on forming students in their own traditions, thereby perpetuating the denomination. They often seem not to have the time, energy, or interest in a broader vision. We encourage seminaries to

3. Church of the Holy Apostles, Harmeyer, interview.

build the capacity for ecumenical engagement and to focus on forming Christians with an ecumenical spirit.

Fr. James Reho, the Episcopal priest serving the Lutheran-Episcopal parish Lamb of God in Fort Myers, suggests that seminarians need to do two things at the same time: to learn one's own tradition "as deeply and intensely" as possible and to "have as wide and diverse an experience of ritual and community and spirituality as one's anxiety level can tolerate." Fr. Reho explains, "those two pieces are equally important because it allows us to speak deeply and authoritatively from our own tradition, but it keeps us pliable enough so that we can work with a tradition in the way where it can be responsive to our world and yet retain its integrity and its life force."[4] Theologically this echoes the doctrine of the Trinity: to witness together to Jesus Christ as fully one, yet in multiple distinctive expressions.

The churches need to encourage and build up those places where there is deep ecumenical engagement. Even in ecumenically situated schools or consortia, there must be opportunities to learn one another's traditions and theologies, such as the Toronto School of Theology, the Washington (DC) Theological Consortium, and the Graduate Theological Union in Berkeley, California. All mainline seminary education in Canada is ecumenical in some way. Yet students often do not learn about the ecumenical movement, or know about local practices of ecumenism, including the presence of ecumenical shared ministry congregations across Canada. The course "Exploring Ecumenical Shared Ministries" at the Saskatoon Theological Union takes students directly into that study. Site visits and internships allow seminarians and ministry candidates to observe and engage with multi-denominational parishes and provide experiential learning that cannot be replicated in the classroom.

BECOMING LITURGICALLY ADEPT AND ADAPTABLE

Particularly important for ecumenical shared ministry is training in the structure of the liturgy of the various traditions represented in the multi-denominational ministry, developing a facility with the liturgical resources and hymnody of other traditions. This requires much more than just learning new hymns. It means mastering the other tradition's liturgical theology and integrating it with one's own—becoming "bi-liturgical," as one early shared ministry practitioner put it.[5] Liturgical theologian and shared ministries pastor Ann Salmon speaks of the need to learn not only the "order" but the "ordo,"

---

4. Lamb of God Church, Reho, interview.

5. Holmes, interview for "Heritage Alive Program."

the deeper structure of a denomination's worship patterns.[6] The presider needs to recognize not only the parts of the liturgy, but also how each part weaves its way into the whole and into the theological heart of the worship service.

The worship leader in a multi-denominational parish offers "a fuller picture of the nature of God at one altar—to hear how God has moved through another person's tradition and experience gives a deeper appreciation of the other, not 'they', but 'we', a part of the family of God."[7] In order for all present to be invited into an ecumenical experience of God, liturgical leaders will not merely know and understand the varying traditions, but also lead the planning and execution of the liturgy to reveal its spiritual dimension and its particular liturgical charisms.

ENCOURAGING AND EMPOWERING LEADERSHIP

A recurrent theme from our interviews is that of positive leadership. The Rev. Ian Twiss emphasizes the importance of "being differentiated."[8] Clergy in this type of ministry need to be open to alternate patterns of governance, new liturgies, different ways of being pastoral to parishioners who come with varied backgrounds and expectations. "Know your tradition, respect your tradition, that's very, very appropriate," another interviewee said. "But keep your arms and your mind open."[9]

Lone-ranger ministry models do not work in multi-denominational parish settings. Clergy serving such parishes need to be open to working with the lay leaders and other clergy who are their partners in ministry. Those who seek these calls must also be equipped for the challenges of coming under the authority of a judicatory not of their own tradition, learning the policies, procedures, regulations, and norms of a different denomination. They must even be able to risk the uncertainty of putting their call on the table when a judicatory leader determines that a parish re-start needs new ministerial leadership.

"Probably the most important thing is for seminarians to admit their frailties, their humanness, their weaknesses, and to serve God, serve Jesus through the church," advises a lay member of a multi-denominational parish.

6. Salmon, "Effect of Worship."

7. Sunriver Christian Fellowship, McGrath-Green, National Lutheran Episcopal Co-ordinating Committee.

8. Holy Faith, Twiss, presentation to Lutheran Episcopal Coordinating Committee.

9. Sunriver Christian Fellowship, Brocker, interview.

"And hopefully that community that you are serving will appreciate and love and respect it."[10]

BEING NON-ANXIOUS MENTORS AND CHANGE AGENTS

Clergy in multi-denominational ministry settings need to be able to function effectively in a system with built-in anxiety, tension, and conflict. The Rev. Judith Ann Roberts, a trained counselor and Fellow in the American Association of Pastoral Counselors as well as an ordained Presbyterian pastor, is a long-term member of Spirit of Grace parish in Hood River, Oregon. She observed two long-established parishes throughout their journey into a shared ministry. From her experience, she suggests, "it would be important for a new seminarian to have previous pastoral experience where there was a lot of conflict, or something that they have to work with in order to keep their head above water, because it is a difficult pastorate."[11] It takes time and intentionality, particularly for the clergy, to foster honest engagement in the parish.[12] The Rev. Laura Hermakin, a longtime pastor serving an Anglican-United Church parish in southern British Columbia, echoes the need to be able to cope with conflict. "They might say it's about the ecumenical sharing, but in the end most conflict has the same roots: 'Nobody listens to me; nobody understands me; nobody loves me.' Recognizing that helps in confronting shared ministry conflict."[13]

Clergy in these settings also need to be discerning about when to lead change and when to follow lay-initiated change. Ministers often are not (and sometimes should not be) the leaders of change. Several interviews recounted experiences with clergy resistant to change as a single-denominational parish moved into a partnership with a parish of another tradition. Laity felt that clergy should "make sure that the people are leading the direction and the pastor is supporting the [lay] leadership."[14] Ministers need to be on board with the changes because they have great power to quash the effort.[15]

10. Sunriver Christian Fellowship, Boubel, interview.

11. Spirit of Grace, Hood River, Richards, interview.

12. Spirit of Grace, West Bloomfield, Campbell, interview.

13. Windermere Valley Shared Ministry, Hermakin, interview.

14. Spirit of Grace, Hood River, Richards, interview.

15. Spirit of Grace, West Bloomfield, Bancroft, interview.

HONORING THE CHARISMS OF MIXED MARRIAGES AND FAMILIES

Laity in ecumenical shared parishes specifically expressed the desire for clergy to understand the difficulties and nurture the gifts of multi-denominational families and marriages. This was especially important to those crossing the Protestant-Catholic boundary (see chapter 3). "I would hope that future clergy would . . . honor the people who come to them for advice or counseling," a member at Holy Apostles Episcopal-Roman Catholic parish said, "so that an ecumenical couple is never told, 'It would be so much easier if one of you would convert.'"[16] A fellow parishioner agreed, "You cannot minister to one half of a couple and expect the other to either see the light or just be ignored. . . . You have to find a way to be more inclusive of that non-Catholic or non-Episcopalian partner."[17] Since over forty percent of the marriages in North America are cross-denominational or multi-religious, pastoral theology courses ought regularly to address the ministry challenges and opportunities of these relationships.

LOVING THE DIVERSE AND PARTICULAR PEOPLE OF GOD

Ecumenical shared parishes incarnate the communion (*koinonia*) of God. At their best, they offer a glimpse of the kingdom of God. It takes a deep and genuine love for the people of God in their diversity and variety and particularity, and a mindset that steadfastly sees that what unites us in Christ is far greater and more significant than what divides us. The minister in Hood River, Oregon, suggests, "The vision that has helped me is really thinking of the strengths that both partners bring to it. Not imagining the congregation as half one thing and half another, but really as 100 percent both. Each denomination and tradition brings these things that are complementary gifts." He encourages his parish to take the time to celebrate those denominational gifts.[18]

While love for the people of God cannot be taught in the classroom, receptivity and relationality are learned through the intensive relationship building and community engagement of an effective seminary education. "People do not remember what you did," a lay leader at Sunriver Christian

---

16. Church of the Holy Apostles, Flowers, interview.

17. Church of the Holy Apostles, Lee Startt, interview.

18. Spirit of Grace, Hood River, King, interview.

Fellowship asserts. "They do not remember what you said. All they remember is how you made them feel. And I feel loved in this congregation."[19]

LIVING THE FAITH RELATIONSHIP WITH GOD

The primary purpose of theological education, according to Methodist historian Justo González, is "to learn how to see everything—including the life of the church—in the light of the word and action of God."[20] This is especially true when the life of the church reflects the diversity and creativity of God. "There are so many God moments in this whole process that you just could not have imagined," said a lay leader at Spirit of Grace in West Bloomfield. "I think for seminarians who are going to be future clergy who would go through this, they have got to . . . really spend a lot of time with God about the whole thing. Just them and God."[21] That individual commitment to prayer and discernment then leads the community of faith to engage together in holy conversations about the parish's life and ministry.

Shared ministry requires an openness to the movement of the Spirit, the call of God, and the example of Jesus Christ: putting God absolutely first. It takes "giving up one's sense of institutional connections," advises one clergyperson, "and a willingness to say, 'Okay, I am here for God, not for a diocese, not for congregation, but for where God is going to lead us.' To put that at the beginning and the end with the whole thing."[22]

EQUIPPED FOR LIFE-LONG FORMATION

Seminaries are not the only place of preparation for shared ministry calls. Experienced clergy who discern a call to serve an ecumenical ministry for a season would benefit from and appreciate a training program. A joint specialized training program similar to intentional interim ministry training could be developed in partner dioceses, synods, and/or conferences. An organized approach is needed for training the lay leaders of parishes merging together as multi-denominational parishes.[23] National church structures could provide a "train the trainers" program for people currently serving in shared ministries at every level: for laypeople, clergy, judiciary leaders, and for seminary facul-

19. Sunriver Christian Fellowship, Bennington, interview.

20. González, *History of Theological Education*, 118.

21. Spirit of Grace, West Bloomfield, Campbell, interview.

22. Spirit of Grace, West Bloomfield, Bancroft, interview.

23. Spirit of Grace, Hood River, Chenoweth, interview.

ty. It is also important to teach bishops and judicatory leaders how to develop these calls, how to administer joint parishes, and how to work collaboratively with other judicatory leaders.

Resources for local ecumenical engagement are needed. Canada's *Ecumenical Shared Ministries Handbook,* prepared by four participating denominations,[24] is a helpful resource, but it is not a formation and training manual. Churches in full communion agreements need to develop study guides for local congregations. National church guidelines for full communion union and federated parishes[25] should be expanded to include practical matters such as worship and sample joint parish covenants.

Education in the twenty-first century must emphasize "creativity, critical thinking, communication, and collaboration; grit, self-motivation, and lifelong learning habits; and entrepreneurship and improvisation—at every level," according to Pulitzer Prize-winning journalist Thomas L. Freidman.[26] These emphases are relevant and needed in theological education today. Formation for ministry should engage evolving new expressions and models of ministry. Multi-denominational ministry is not for every seminarian and clergyperson; it takes a special vocation for this work. But ecumenical partnerships can be an unparalleled opportunity for ministerial service for those with an ecumenical vocation. Beauty and holiness are to be found in the rich variety of expressions of faith and experiences of God in multi-denominational parish ministry.

24. *Ecumenical Shared Ministries Handbook.*
25. Evangelical Lutheran Church in America, "Documents of Governance and Policy."
26. Friedman, *Thank You for Being Late,* 212.

11

Do You Have to Be Something?

Multiple Belonging

IT WAS A ROUTINE episcopal confirmation visitor—as routine as a trip to a shared ministry in a northern resource company town can be. The bishop had arrived by plane, and was sitting in the cheery living room of the local lay reader, drinking tea with her, the non-Anglican pastor, the four Anglican confirmands, and their parents. After some pleasant conversation, the bishop asked if anyone had any questions.

"I do," said a young mother, a certain edge in her voice. "My son does not like having to choose a denomination."

"Is this true?" the bishop turned to the twelve-year-old.

"Yes," he agreed. "I belong to St. —. I don't want to have to be only Anglican."

"Me too," said another confirmand. "We just want to be Christian!" The other confirmands joined the chorus: "Why can't we just be confirmed as Christians?"

"But you can't do that," said the bishop, nervously picking the white hair of the lay reader's cat off his black cassock. "You can't just be Christians. You have to be *something*."[1]

The bishop, the children, and their parents had just confronted one of the challenges of multi-denominational ministry: such congregations live in a liminal space. Like the kingdom of God itself, they live an ecumenical reality that is "already but not yet." Roman Catholic ecumenical theology speaks of

---

1. This is an actual event; names and location have been withheld.

dwelling in a "real but imperfect communion." Much of the time, an ecumenical parish experiences the "reality" of unity and shared life. Then again, and certainly at confirmation, the "not yet," the "imperfect," surges to the fore. In so doing, it highlights both the absurdities of disunity and the intractability of challenging that disunity. Surely, the first apostles were "just Christians." When they tried to be something other—to belong to Cephas or Apollos—Paul excoriated them: "Has Christ been divided?" (1 Cor 1:13). To demand a Christian be "something" implies faithful discipleship in community is not enough.

Yet, many Christians would argue that one *does* have to be "something." As *The Church: Towards a Common Vision* puts it, "Each local church . . . is wholly Church, but not the whole Church. . . . This communion of local churches is thus not an optional extra."[2] If a local congregation does not have defined links with the wider church, it is in danger of existing only for itself, for "belonging to Cephas" rather than to the world. In the churches' still-divided state, the faithful believer, in addition to being Christian, needs a community, or "tribe," to which to belong.

This insistence upon relationship with the wider church helps to set multi-denominational congregations apart from "non-denominational" and "community" churches. Multi-denominational congregations acknowledge the historic gifts of their participating traditions and the ongoing nurture, oversight, and connection they provide. As a teenager in an ecumenical shared congregation described it, "Being affiliated with denominations gives the congregation some accountability. Affiliation shows that the church is helping out in the world."[3] However, multi-denominational congregations also pose challenges to the blemishes that mar the face of Christian unity, to the "imperfect" and the "not yet" with which many Christians live so complacently. Membership is one of the most obvious of these challenges. Participating churches do little to assist with this question. Even full communion agreements—which give extensive attention to the exchangeability of ordained ministries, and assert that "communicant members of each church" are "able freely to communicate at the altar of the other," and are to be received in one church with the same status they had in the other[4]—do not specify how membership occurs in shared parishes.

This chapter explores the ways that ecumenical shared ministry congregations and their denominations have struggled with the question of

---

2. *Church: Towards a Common Vision*, §31.

3. St. Peter's Ecumenical Church, name withheld, interview.

4. See, for example, National Convention of the Evangelical Lutheran Church, "Called to Full Communion," Declaration of Full Communion commentary.

membership in the Body of Christ, either by celebrating the opportunity to choose their denominational membership or by seeking ways to "push the envelope" around Christian identity and belonging. We then look at the underlying issues involved in membership and belonging, and ask if multi-denominational congregations are, in fact, challenging the "branding" that is so prevalent in contemporary American and Canadian Christianity.

CHOOSING TO CHOOSE

Not all confirmands in multi-denominational ministries are hostile to the notion of making a denominational choice. The Rev. Leigh Sinclair discusses her theology of confirmation and membership:

> It actually helped that the confirmands had to make a decision about which church to be confirmed in. My personal confirmation theology is that it is time for you to take responsibility for the vows taken at baptism. It is a way to help them take ownership—if you choose United Church, then you have to take responsibility for being part of that church. A fourth-generation Anglican, who really wanted to be confirmed "ecumenical," went home and talked to his grandmother. She said to him, "This gives you an opportunity to be the fourth generation of your family confirmed Anglican in Slave Lake." That is impressive. It was about claiming their heritage.[5]

Multi-denominational members speak of the opportunity to research their roots, and to explore the two or more identities available to them within their own congregation. One woman describes her decision this way. "I was raised in a family that did not go to church. . . . When I was confirmed [as an adult in an multi-denominational congregation] I wondered why I could not just be a child of God. But I did decide to be Lutheran, because I liked the tradition and my Danish Lutheran roots."[6]

Young people do not necessarily resist denominational membership. "I feel like I am the kid of a blended family. . . . I do feel really comfortable in my Disciples setting. But I have also worked with United Church conferences," said one.[7] Said another, "I am not confused about who I am as a Christian."[8] "It has been a benefit to our family," explained a mother of four children who

5. St. Peter's Ecumenical Church, Sinclair, interview.

6. St. Peter's Ecumenical Church, Anderson, interview.

7. St. Peter's Ecumenical Church , name withheld, interview.

8. Broadway Disciples United, Marcelino, interview.

were raised in two different multi-denominational congregations. "We can pull on a multitude of traditions. . . . Families don't have to select one tradition and leave the rest behind."[9] At Indian Hill Church in Cincinnati, the youth director leads confirmation classes. While the objective is to understand the basics of the Apostles' Creed, confirmands are encouraged to choose one or the other membership designation by confirmation day. Indian Hill is home to several Presbyterian/Episcopal families.

Some youth who come from a Presbyterian family choose to be confirmed Episcopalian because of the liturgy's impact on them. Alternatively, a young person from an Episcopal family might choose the Presbyterian identity out of identification with its Reformed theology or in honor of an influential family member from that tradition. Some worshipers in multi-denominational congregations, then, appreciate having the opportunity of investigating the participating traditions, and choosing one to which to belong, while staying within the fellowship that nurtured them.[10] These Christians find the gift of diversity that is the unintended legacy of the church's disunity. The service of confirmation, like those described in chapter 7, can be a moment not to despair over the churches' divisions, but to celebrate the foretaste of unity multi-denominational congregations represent.

PUSHING THE MEMBERSHIP ENVELOPE

Others, like the children who wanted just to "be Christians," see the necessity of choosing a denomination to be retrogressive, giving in to the church's brokenness. For many young people, "there is nothing else but both."[11] People are attracted to multi-denominational congregations precisely because its witness is not as narrowly defined. "People can come to this church because it's not 'just this.' There is freedom in that," one laywoman explained.[12] A young woman commented that "people my age are not interested in denominations,"[13] echoing much contemporary literature about North American Christianity.[14]

A few multi-denominational congregations push the membership envelope by flying beneath the radar—a blended liturgy, music from eclectic sources, generic confirmation classes and liturgies (or just let the Anglican

9. St. Peter's Ecumenical Church, name withheld, interview.

10. Indian Hill Church, Caine, interview.

11. Broadway Disciples United, Cuthbert, interview.

12. St. Peter's Ecumenical Church, Marge Procyshyn, interview.

13. St. Peter's Ecumenical Church, name withheld, interview.

14. An early example is Roof, *Spiritual Marketplace*.

bishop confirm everyone), and generally downplay their denominational ties. One family chose their denominations when they received the "long form" of the Canadian census—which requires specificity around religious adherence. While ecumenical shared congregations that quietly eschew denominational identities are rare, there have been attempts to resist "forced choice" membership in more overt ways. Churches Together in England is an ecumenically sponsored organization that promotes and supports local ecumenical ministries. Its standards for multi-denominational ministries (called "Local Ecumenical Partnerships") allows for persons in these ministries to be members of *all* of the fully participating denominations.[15] Similarly, at Indian Hill Church, there was a time when confirmands had the option to choose to be both Presbyterian and Episcopalian, and Presbyterian and Episcopal clergy, including the bishop, laid hands on them simultaneously. More recently, the diocesan bishop has asked candidates to choose a single identity at confirmation.[16]

While the practice of multiple membership might play havoc with church and state census takers, it recognizes the deep ecumenical integrity of the multi-denominational experience. Those who have been formed in two or more denominational worldviews do experience themselves as hybrids, belonging to more than one tradition. At the same time, such official multiple belonging also acknowledges the distinctiveness of the participating traditions. It does not pretend that one can be an unhyphenated Christian in the present state of divided churches. At some point, those with multiple membership may have to choose a denomination in which to become more active as a layperson, or to pursue an ordered ministry. Even then, they should be able to do so without forsaking other aspects of their Christian identity. If the churches really do respect "unity in diversity," is there a reason they should not respect the "diversity" that might exist in the "unity" of an individual's formation and commitment?

MEMBERSHIP, IDENTITY, AND BRANDING

Denominational identities run deep in the Christian experience. In the 1980s, the Anglican-Reformed International Commission sought to understand the roots of denominational attachments, as they saw them in some ways as impediments to unity.

> General obstacles to unity include the fear that union means loss of identity. This fear goes very deep. No one becomes a Christian,

15. Churches Together in England, "Model Governing Document."
16. Indian Hill Church, Caine, interview.

and no one grows up into mature Christian discipleship, except through forms of teaching, worship, practice, and piety, which have been developed in a particular tradition. . . . When the encounter takes place with a Christian nurtured in another tradition, there arises the painful necessity of going beyond and behind the received form to a new apprehension of the substance—of the presence of Christ himself. This is a kind of fresh conversion. It cannot be easy. It should not surprise us that it is resisted with passionate intensity, because resistance seems to be required by fidelity to Christ as he has made himself known to us in the past.[17]

Those who have come to multi-denominational ministry from other Christian experiences speak of that "fresh conversion"—and we have heard their voices throughout the pages of this book. Others have been nurtured in multiple traditions, and for them "going beyond and behind the received form" is not a "painful necessity" but a natural part of belonging to a "blended family." However, the story is different in the church beyond multi-denominational ministries. Most mainstream denominations in the United States and Canada operate from a narrative that sees the churches under threat from a secular, disinterested culture. In this fraught context, denominational identities—rather than developing softer edges and permeable boundaries—have become a way to create distinctions and foster loyalty. We might call this need to highlight denominational distinctiveness the "branding" of Christian identities.

There is a growing literature linking religious communities and "branding," a concept that has blossomed in global capitalism.[18] Corporations spend vast sums of money and human capital to market, not simply products, but also "brands." A brand is not the product, but the essence of what the product seeks to represent. A company cannot rest on its product, since many products are almost indistinguishable from each other, so it sets itself apart by its "brand." Research shows that customers are typically more willing to pay higher prices for branded products than for unknown brands, in no small part because a chip in the human brain has responded emotionally to brand advertising. Corporate "branding" increasingly uses the language previously reserved for religious communities: it speaks to the spirit, essence, or soul of a product. As Naomi Klein writes in her anti-branding manifesto, *No Logo*,

17. Anglican-Reformed International Commission, *God's Reign and Our Unity*, par. 12.

18. Some examples of this literature include: Einstein, *Brands of Faith*; Twitchell, *Branded Nation*; and Usunier and Stolz, *Religions as Brands*.

"Advertizing is about hawking a product. Branding, in its truest and most advanced incarnations, is about corporate transcendence."[19]

Sure enough, in order for faith communities, which might appear quite similar to outsiders, to survive in a time of indifference to traditional confessional allegiances, church leaders see a need to "brand" them, and to teach members to practice "brand loyalty." For example, the Anglican Church of Canada reports, under the headline "Congregational Development: On the Rediscovery of Anglican Identity," on the work of Bishop Melissa Skelton. "Skelton now champions what she found to be a nearly universal quality of developing congregations—"the rediscovery of this thing we called an Anglican ethos, Anglican spirituality, Anglican identity." She recognizes "deepening ecclesial identity" as one of the five core factors in developing strong congregations.[20]

Sociologists place no overt judgment on these practices, but they do paint an unflattering social picture. "Religious leaders," writes British quantitative sociologist David Voas, "face the sort of challenge familiar to cigarette manufacturers. It is not enough to show that the product is good of its kind; the brand manager must overcome some resistance to the kind of thing it is. Fairly or unfairly," says Voas, "religion has come to be associated with a number of unpopular things."[21] Thus, in order to clarify their role, religions, including Christianity, are propelled into the marketplace by multiple social and economic forces. Our denominations develop attractive websites. They labor over logos and image. Congregations and denominations are encouraged to develop their niche, to name what sets them apart and might make them attractive to spiritual consumers.

The branding emphasis presents a challenge to ecumenical shared ministries. One might suggest these congregations are simply examples of "co-branding," since they offer several brands, rather than one. Marketing research reveals complicated outcomes when advertising attempts to "co-brand" products. Most interesting for denominational "branding" is the finding that those with strong emotional attachments to a brand are more likely to be troubled to see their product co-branded with another. In one experiment, the informants "felt humiliated by the brand alliance."[22] It may be, then, that judicatories, clergy, and some laypersons—those whose daily lives are enmeshed with their denominational identity—are more apt to be anxious about the "co-branding" inherent in multi-denominational congregations than church

19. Klein, *No Logo*, 21.

20. Gardner, "Congregational Development."

21. David Voas, Preface, in Usunier and Stolz, *Religions as Brands*, xvii.

22 Xiao and Wan, "Co-Branding with an Emotional Brand," 902.

"shoppers" might be. The participants in ecumenical shared ministries often wish to resist the language of branding altogether. Some consider it important that they weaken the focus on the denominational "brand." As the Rev. Ray Cuthbert of Broadway Disciples United in Winnipeg put it, "It's telling the world that we are about Christ and not about a denominational shingle." He goes on to suggest that in fact, "branding" is a problem, not a solution.

> The problem with the larger mainline churches is that they always see themselves as the beginning and the end, and they can't see themselves as being anything but that. . . . They are not willing to envision something other than what they've known. . . . They are used to being self-reliant. They are not used to a notion that we must work ecumenically in order to bring the witness of Christ into this day and age with the resources we've got.[23]

François Prévost of St. Peter's Ecumenical Church believes denominational leaders can exhibit "a misplaced pride" in their own tradition.[24] Multi-denominational congregations generally seek to put Christian identity before denominational identity. Another St. Peter's member, Janice Nowichin says, "I think the biggest lesson that I have learned, that I would want others to experience is that first and foremost at St. Peter's we are Christians; our denominations come second."[25] In that regard, these ecumenically shared congregations stand as a countersign to the "branding" impetus. In their complex but real relationship with multiple traditions, they encourage conversion that does not deny denominational heritage, but always puts it at the service of a more significant one—being a follower of Jesus Christ.

"Why can't we just be Christians?" the confirmands implored the bishop. Multi-denominational congregations live on the edge of that perplexing question.

23. Broadway Disciples United, Cuthbert, interview.
24. St. Peter's Ecumenical Church, Prévost, interview.
25. St. Peter's Ecumenical Church, Nowichin, interview.

12

Keeping the Faith
Ecclesiology

MUCH HAS BEEN SAID about "the Other" in late modern and postmodern thought—the not-self, he/she/it who is not "I," whose experiences, thought world, and self-understanding are different from that of the self by dint of *not being* the self. The Other may be of a different gender, race, sexual orientation, nationality, political ideology, or religious belonging. What effect does this indeterminate "other" have upon the presumably known self? To what extent may this other even come to define or alter the "I," thus exposing the self's permeability and contingency, or, perhaps, revealing the subject's true self, thus becoming indispensable for the subject's intelligibility? These are some questions the other poses to the self.[1]

Now, is it such a stretch to see not only individuals, but a kind of corporate "self" represented in theological traditions and denominations, each with unique histories, understandings, habits, and "personal" crises? Institutions, like people, have distinct provenances, growing pains, identity crises, internal dissonances, and aging processes. If you can imagine this, then unique Christian traditions-as-selves are replete with all the identity and internal contradictions had by a single human being. Imagine, then, how human beings

---

1. The philosophical discussion of this question has centered in the twentieth century around options posed by Emanuel Levinas, Gabriel Marcel, Martin Buber, Jaques Derrida, and Paul Ricoeur. The differing positions of Levinas and Marcel contribute to our framework. See Levinas, *Totality and Infinity*; and Marcel, *Mystery of Being*, 2 vols., but the more immediate theological inspiration comes from Miroslav Volf's treatment of otherness in *Exclusion and Embrace*.

encounter one another, strike up friendships, find themselves sharing living space, and perhaps marrying. Churches do, too.

What might the particular sort of togetherness ecumenical shared ministries have meant, theologically, more specifically, ecclesiologically? This chapter contributes a framework for an ecclesiology for the local ecumenical shared ministry. In short, multi-denominational congregations need an ecclesiology accounting for "otherness" in particular ways other churches do not. From there, other key factors in "regular" local church self-understandings, such as identity and hospitality, come into play in unique ways for ecumenical ministries. As the book title indicates and this chapter contends, the sort of ecclesiology they practice is *daring*.

WHAT IS ECCLESIOLOGY?

Asking "What is a local ecumenical church?" requires the prior question, "What is *church?*" That is the question of ecclesiology: the nature and function of the church as such. Ecumenists and those who live out their faith ecumenically must face the question, and they have a rich collection of models and perspectives from across the ecclesial spectrum with which to think. Beginning with the New Testament, we find some provisional thinking about the church's nature. Paul and other writers grappled with something like ecclesiology when addressing the dilemmas of a church comprised of Jews and Gentiles of varying beliefs and socioeconomic backgrounds (1 Cor 1:12; 11:18–21). Prominent in Paul's efforts to convince the Corinthians they were not quite doing church right is his notion of *koinonia*, usually translated "fellowship," and it has become a pervasive and inviting descriptor of the church ever since. Congregations are places of fellowship. There are fellowship hours on Sunday mornings in fellowship halls. People join churches, appealing to the warm "fellowship" they experience. Who could possibly be against fellowship? However, our assumptions about the word *koinonia* as "fellowship," referring to the warm feeling of togetherness or mutual goodwill, is not actually what Paul and other New Testament writers had in mind when they used the word in their writings. Leaving aside the question of the term's secular or sacred origins,[2] *koinonia* is "participation in something," sharing, or partnership, not "fellowship" or association as such, which are the *results* of participation.[3] Someone (e.g., Jesus) or a quality might be the proper objects of participation.

2. Campbell, "KOINONIA and Its Cognates," argues for its secular usage, borrowed by Paul and other NT writers.

3. Campbell, "KOINONIA and Its Cognates," 352–80; Neufeld, "Koinonia," 341.

Paul's use of *koinonia* was in connection with, for instance, Jesus, (1 Cor 1:9), participation in offering for the Jerusalem church (1 Cor 16:1–4), or participation in Eucharist (1 Cor 10:16). The word also appears in a more strictly ecclesial sense in 1 John 1:3–7; Acts 2:42, where it indicates sharing together in the trinitarian life and in apostolic ministry, respectively.

What is the common core around which the people participate in a multi-denominational congregation? What are we doing together? And, why *must* we do it together? These are helpful questions for ecumenical shared ministries in search of an ecclesiological basis for their existence. Longitudinal, ecumenical togetherness is not simply for the joy it may bring, though that is part of the appeal and the yield. It is surely for the purpose set by Jesus' high priestly prayer. To be in *koinonia* is to be gathered around all that can be gathered around. For certain shared congregations that will mean Word and sacrament, others only Word, or common convictions, juridical structures shared in part or whole—so that oneness can be lived out and a witness made to the church's true nature. The extent to which this is possible in any given ecumenical combination depends upon standards set forth in full communion documents, by regional judicatories, or by local constitutional/covenant stipulations.

The Corinthian church was a cantankerous bunch. With its headstrong factions all part of one body but often at odds, maybe it was a kind of accidental multi-denominational congregation! They quarreled over a laundry list of theological matters: the Lord's Supper, glossolalia, the role of women, marriage, ministry, idols, and equality. Scholar Dale Martin argues a number of these Christians, particularly the wealthier among them, mimicked forms of hierarchy found in Greco-Roman society and applied them to the church.[4] As they imagined it, the authentic believers were at the top, naturally most capable of controlling the "body" below, full of parts and factions with lesser understanding corresponding to lesser social status. The "strong" (e.g., socially advantaged and spiritually "fit") looked down upon the "weak" (e.g., slaves, non-tongues speakers) and established a spiritual pecking order that reflected worldly standards. Paul, says Martin, joined these "low status" believers in rejecting a hierarchical body for a permeable one in which all, not just some, were vulnerable to outside assaults from a hostile culture and interior propensities to engage in mutual blame and backbiting. He effectively turned the body of the church on its side to avoid privileging one faction over another, or to invite feelings of superiority on the part of another. This view of the church as body assumed one answer coming from one group within it, threatening the community. Instead of being "called out," the church simply

4. Martin, *Corinthian Body*.

mirrored Greco-Roman society and fought within itself in the name of being impervious to dissention and strife. The church's unity was being imperiled by hierarchical social relations its members brought with them into the church from the Greco-Roman world.[5]

Martin argues that Paul saw how church unity requires a status-reversal between self and other. There is a modern analog to the Corinthian problem in old denominational rivalries where the convictions and practices of the other are continually subject to failing the scrutiny of the normative self, and vice-versa. To have one's tradition permeated by too much of the other (as in "That practice is too Catholic," or "Those are Baptist songs!") is thought to threaten boundaries and hierarchies of truth, a permeability that might literally threaten the ecclesial body's "health."[6] The natural (or, we might say, sinful) propensity to prioritize self (insider) over other (outsider) is turned on its side in an ecumenical fellowship in which both groups are "other" to the partner and the two cannot be in a relationship of normative to hetero-normative, as an individual congregation might think of itself in relationship to another down the street. Hence, the two bodies become permeable to one another, open to exchange and reception of goods from each tradition.[7] Fellowship comes through being called together by the Spirit to share goods in common, but, if the Corinthians have anything to teach ecumenists, this can be a challenge to established norms and comfort levels.

Another ecclesiological possibility receiving much attention lately is offered in *communio* ecclesiology. Orthodox theologian John Zizioulas has largely contributed to this approach. The starting point is the Trinity, in which "God" does not name a being prior to the trinitarian persons in relationship to one another, but rather *is* those relationships each person has to the others. All being, human or divine, is in communion with other beings; there is no such thing as a detached being, and, inasmuch as humans attempt to do so, they sin in rebellion against the communal God and their own communal selves. Personhood, with its uniqueness and gifts, entails the capacity for communion, both in God and humans. It is individuation, or being over-against others that, for Zizioulas, names a distorted view of God and the nature of human sin. Ecclesially, humans become whole selves after the image of the Trinity and in *koinonia* around the church's constitutive event, the Eucharistic celebration.[8]

---

5. Martin, *Corinthian Body*, especially Part I, "Hierarchy."

6. Martin suggests this in a slightly different connection in Part II of his book.

7. O'Gara, *Ecumenical Gift Exchange*.

8. Zizioulas, *Being As Communion*, 86–89, 101–5. For a summary of Zizioulas' work, see Kärkkäinen, *Introduction to Ecclesiology*, 95–102.

The church as trinitarian body is, to be sure, Christ's body, but, to say so always implies its indwelling by the Father and the Spirit (in classic Eastern fashion, the Son and Spirit each proceed from the Father). The church is a creature of the Trinity. It is not the case that there is first the church and then the Spirit's blessing. Nor is it true for this view that Christ and the Spirit are disjoined, a dilemma Zizioulas sees as the theological source of the rift between local and universal. The Spirit is the heart of the church's being. Such constitution checks the overemphasis on juridical and hierarchical structures to which the church is often prone, and draws attention to the local assembly where the church's fullness exists, with bishop and people gathered around the eucharist. One and many (Christ and his body; bishop and assembly) are two sides to the church's one coin.[9]

The myriad forms of human otherness is an invitation to *koinonia*, or full personhood on the part of all humanity, but which is realized fully in the church. Though ecumenicity is not among them, Zizoulas addresses a catalog of the kinds of human otherness found in the church, such as gender, race, and economic status. The human otherness that invites relatedness leads to mutual and reciprocal self-giving, as does God's economic trinitarian life.[10]

Other theologians have taken up the theme of intra-trinitarian relatedness as an ecclesiological model. Colin Gunton and Miroslav Volf, for instance, both formulate Trinitarian ecclesiologies in Protestant contexts.[11] Multi-denominational congregations can find *communio* ecclesiology useful, especially if they regularly share eucharist together. Zizioulas offers ample reflections for those for whom sacramental *koinonia* is central to worship and self-understanding.[12]

Other models abound. Is the church finally a mystical body that transcends institutional forms? Is it primarily the People of God, as the Second Vatican Council made foundational to its work? Or is it a body called together by the preaching of the Word? Is it at once both righteous by grace and sinful by nature? Is it an eschatological reality that has not yet come to be in its fullness, but about which we get glimpses, perhaps most vividly where Christians of different stripes gather? Many shared ministry constituents attest to the proleptic character of their churches: it is a present harbinger of the kingdom not present, a signpost to the future of God's reign.

---

9. Zizioulas, *Being As Communion*, 132–39.

10. Harrison, "Zizioulas on Communion and Otherness," 280.

11. Gunton, *Promise of Trinitarian Theology*; Volf, *After Our Likeness*; Ingle-Gillis, *Trinity and Ecumenical Church*. For a liberation ecclesiology, see Boff, *Holy Trinity*.

12. Thiessen, *Ecumenical Ecclesiology*, see especially essays in Part II.

Do any of these models fit the multi-denominational parish context? In a sense, they all do. While there is something useful about each one, finally, we propose that an ecclesiology for multi-denominational congregations best emerges from the stories such as are related in this study, told from the grassroots, and built out of the experience of assembling, not just week after week under one roof, but with attention to the circumstances under which the local congregation embarked upon the common journey. What brought them together? No matter how lofty or mundane the answer, there was some element of bravery, of daring, that made it happen. The ecclesiology argued for here, while made of elements of *koinonia, communio,* and others, is finally a unique one: *an ecclesiology based on a dare.*

DARING ECCLESIOLOGY

What makes a multi-denominational congregation a daring proposition? Is it the delicate task of combining resources, with the possibility that some treasured habits and assets might be cast aside in the interests of unity? Is it the possibility of failure? Will people respond to the ecumenical "brand," or find it confusing? Will the warm sun of federation end in a discouraging ecumenical winter of failure?

These congregations require bravery and daring because engagement with otherness—even among Christians—unleashes the potential for disagreement, the clash of doctrines, polities, liturgies, and sensibilities taken for granted in one household and frowned upon in another. And all this despite carefully worked out ecumenical agreements! Ecumenical agreements often look appealing and promising on paper. Theologians worked hard on them. But transferring theological consensus from paper to shared life is a daunting step, a move from the conceptual to the existential. Liturgies may be practically identical and governing boards may operate similarly, but the high-minded goals of ecumenism seem to wither when it comes down to which set of paraments to use or questions about the Sunday School curriculum's theological nuance. People—clergy included—begin to ask if this can be done. Some may end up seeking out a parish purely of their denomination. Others might slip out the back door and become inactive. Some clergy, once idealistic, might seek other opportunities less encumbered by the extra weight brought by an ecumenical arrangement.

Though the dare surely involves all of these risks, it is daring because every step, every decision, every delicate task involves an "other." It is daring because, in cases where the partners belong to denominations that are in full communion as the result of decades of patient dialog, the proof must now be in the pudding: does what sounds good on paper actually work? The "other" may be a divergent theological tradition, full of insistent or preferred liturgical particularities; different forms of clergy deployment; or even variant Christian educational curriculum. Despite difference, two or more traditions, while not ceasing to be fully themselves, come together to share all they possibly can in the close quarters of shared resources: buildings, budgets, constitutions, and clergy. If it is difficult enough in the current milieu to launch a new parish start, how much more a federated congregation.

Ecumenism requires an ethic of prioritizing the other over the self's propensity to colonize and dominate. So, as an Episcopalian in a Lutheran–Episcopal shared ministry, I commit to being an Episcopalian so that my Lutheran brethren can find themselves by me being me, which would be impossible if I/we were to homogenize into a lowest common denominator, or mere pluralism. I cannot fashion my partner after my own image or my perception of her; she must be allowed her otherness, which in fact makes communion possible, a being together around shared gifts. As ecumenist Michael Kinnamon notes, "The church dare not be a community of like individuals who affirm each other; rather, it must be a community of unlike individuals who know themselves to be affirmed together by the grace of God."[13] Multi-denominational congregations exist to witness to denominational identity as that which, along with race, gender, economic status, and every other particularity, must be reconciled in the unity that Christ creates out of the church.

The dare begins in the encounter, whether in the initial bravery of forming an ecumenical congregation or sustaining the relationship over decades. Faced with the threat of closure, some congregations combine out of financial need more than with the dare of a new self-understanding. What might have begun out of temporal necessity often ends up becoming a theological necessity in the hearts and minds of constituents. "Why didn't we do this long before?" they ask.

This relationship is sustained in a paradox of separability and inseparability.[14] As long as specific ecclesial identities endure in the shared ministry, there is separability, individuation, specific characteristics at play. As long as discrete ecclesial identities are in communion, doing ministry together under one roof, they are drawn together by the Spirit in mutual inseparability,

---

13. Kinnamon, *Truth and Community*, 7.

14. Much of the inspiration for this paragraph is from Veling, "For You Alone."

an "unrelenting relation" in Levinas' words.[15] In one sense, the individuation respective traditions provide points to the wounded human creation, couched in our estrangement into competing groups that fetishize group identity and thematize the other in terms not her own. Church disunity is caused by, and shares in, human sinfulness, the turning away from God and neighbor. In that sense, it is "unnatural."

Yet, looked at as an imperfect sign of the Spirit's gift of diversity to the one church, church disunity can be a stunningly beautiful thing, even an enablement of the very unity it lacks. The nature of true unity, according to the Spirit's gifts and the diversity of the biblical canon (to name one instance of primal diversity), requires otherness. Whether in Paul's day or ours, there is no church unity based on mere uniformity, or the collapse of other and self into undifferentiated oneness.

To take an example from historical theology: in mysticism (at least varieties that were not declared heretical) the aim is not for the self to be absorbed into the Divine, but to be in communion with it. When the self is in communion with God, gone is all that would separate the self from God, while the self at the same time becomes most fully self, released from chains, self-imposed or otherwise. This is love of God, mystics say. Love of neighbor, which Jesus always paralleled, is inseparable from this God-self relationship and thus rests on the same sort of communion. I do not dissolve into my neighbor any more than I remain his or her enemy. I have relinquished a lesser self-understanding created in isolation from others for a greater self, found only with others. In my communion with neighbor I am free to be myself.

Moreover, there are material benefits that accrue to mutual otherness under one roof. For one, sameness would render growth impossible. The self cannot grow in self-awareness in the absence of a different other. There would be no learning, no exchange, no mutual correction and enrichment, no built-in, resident challenge from otherness with which to be inspired or challenged, and nothing to contemplate (save perhaps navels). In short, isolation leaves little capacity for relationship, and thus, a sort of ontological violence is done to creation. The love—the very being of God—requires communion with another, as the *communio* ecclesiologists have shown. I cannot love you if I have reduced you to me.[16]

What follows is an extended architectural metaphor that might illustrate what a daring ecclesiology looks like based on where it happens. The Spirit's daring, risky business of bringing divided Christians together under one roof

15. Levinas, *Totality and Infinity*, 295.

16. Emmanuel Levinas and Richard Kearney, "Dialogue with Emmanuel Levinas," in Cohen, *Face to Face*, 22.

invites comparison with innovations in other arenas about the use of space which, while hopefully true of any sort of church life, offers clues to the profundity of the dare of ecumenical *koinonia*. Finally, this daring ecclesiology's Christological basis will round out the discussion.

ECUMENICAL ARCHITECTURE

Nothing quite illustrates unity-in-diversity than the *Simultankirchen*, found in parts of Europe and mentioned in the Introduction. These Catholic-Protestant structures sometimes featured two altars, placed side by side, with architectural features and symbols to differentiate them. And so, when the dare has been made, and two or more, without ceasing to be such, become one, there must be a place for this to happen. Shared space, at the heart of the multi-denominational experience, provides an apt metaphor for daring ecclesiology. Each "other" breaks out of congregational silos and denominational echo chambers to share ministry together. This is a constant among ecumenical churches. Not that any local church, single or ecumenical, must own a building, but the symbolism of the shared assembly space invites reflection on ecumenical ecclesiology for its wealth of metaphors. It takes a foundation, walls, and a roof to make a building, and so it does for a multi-denominational congregation.

Buildings are made of walls and roofs, suggestive of boundaries and covering, particulars (walled off spaces) and universals (roofs covering an entire structure). People inhabit the space created by walls and roofs, and the people in a multi-denominational congregation are, as with any human gathering or Christian congregation, an assemblage of "others."

For one to be with another, the one—"I," "we,"—must by definition be discrete, an identity made exclusive by a boundary. I cannot be with you by merging into you. I must be me, a subject, before I can be with you. Philosopher Emmanuel Levinas's notion of the subject applies here where he explains that the self must be allowed to be as such without being co-opted by the self's interlocutor. I do not narrate my friend's story for her; she describes herself in her own words. At the center of the self is a reality that cannot be fully known by the other, and thus cannot be intruded upon, "colonized," or franchised. The other is other.[17] And so, there are rightfully walls. Boundaries still matter.

Yet, walls by themselves are too much. They prevent or destroy relationships. They often prevent seeing, usually hearing, and always touching. "Belonging without distance destroys. . . . But distance without belonging

---

17. Levinas, *Totality and Infinity*, 13.

isolates."[18] When one church declares itself to be the "one true church," it has declared its self-sufficiency for inspiration and correction, and runs the danger of creating its own purity cult whose congress with Christians beyond the walls is fraught with anxiety about theological, ethical, or liturgical "contamination." Life behind a wall can comfortably lull the enclosed into a false security. With not unlike metaphor, Jesus seemed to be addressing a similar problem with the Pharisees when he said, "But woe to you, scribes and Pharisees, hypocrites! For you lock people out of the kingdom of heaven. For you do not go in yourselves, and when others are going in, you stop them" (Matt 23:13). The fine balance is between boundaries and connections, communion and otherness, so that the walls do not collapse bringing the unifying roof down. Nor leaving the walls without windows, doors, and the possibility of open spaces not even marked by walls.

Architects have given us other ways to illustrate difference and belonging with popular "open floor plan" homes, in which the kitchen, dining, and living areas once walled off from each other are now differentiated with other markers besides walls. Family, guests, and pets might find themselves all in one space whose functions are distinguished by, perhaps, floor treatments— carpet, wood, tile, linoleum. Colors and furniture compliment and contrast at the same time and in the same field of vision. Functions in one part of the room, such as cooking, are provided for, but the kitchen space maintains its function and integrity while "generously" open to the living area in the room's opposite corner. Guests and cooks talk across an open counter: the cook preparing a meal for the sake of the guests, the guests invited by the open space to lend their aid to the cook. Many of the multi-denominational congregations studied in this book function more like homes with open floor plans than houses with traditional, wall-bounded rooms. In any case, boundaries make discrete identities and differences possible, to be celebrated and enjoyed. Different identities make relationships possible.[19]

The concept of "shared space" has also come in vogue in urban planning as a way to create streetscapes better shared by people and cars. Erase curbs and distinctions between sidewalks and streets, and as a consequence, designers find that cars slow down, accidents are reduced, with a sense that cars and pedestrians share the same space, cars not controlling or threatening the usage of the space. Apply this to church buildings, and the sense that one group is the "real owner" of the place is replaced by a freedom to live together with constant attention to the other, and what must be done to be "in communion" in ways that live up to ecumenical ideals. Of course, there is a risk involved

18. Volf, *Exclusion and Embrace*, 50.

19. Volf, *Exclusion and Embrace*, 67.

in open floor plans, streetscapes, and commonly held ecclesial space. It is the dare of sharing without ceasing to be fully oneself, nor asking the other to cease being herself. It is the dare of being vulnerable to the possibility that I might be changed, challenged, and transformed by my partner in ways out of my control or expectation.

Therefore, this is all a matter of hospitality. It means welcoming the stranger, the other, as the companion. If the traditions involved stand on an equal footing, sharing the space, then they are to welcome one another (Rom 15:7). The posture adopted to the outsider must be shared among the insiders, even of different stripes. Susan Durber preached:

> [An] important thing about the biblical view of hospitality is that it's as important to receive it as to give it. We can very easily imagine that God wants the Church to be hospitable, welcoming, and inclusive. We can readily think of the Church as "host." But it's interesting, isn't it, that of all those countless stories about Jesus sharing meals with his disciples, with Pharisees, with tax-collectors, with whoever it was, he was not the host, but pretty much always the guest. Jesus was the stranger who was welcomed. He was the one who received hospitality—and it was in that way that he found a place to offer the welcome of God. He did not invite people to enter his space on his terms—he willingly entered their homes, their space, their communities, and laid himself open to them. Whether you think of Jesus eating with the disreputable, or with those disciples at Emmaus, he was the guest, receiving what was offered. And when he asked the disciples to follow him, he didn't suggest that they had open house or offered hospitality to guests, but he sent them out in such a vulnerable condition that they would have to rely on the hospitality of others. Jesus sent his disciples out—without spare clothes, without a stick to lean on, completely vulnerable. To be a disciple is to be open to receive hospitality and vulnerable enough to need it.[20]

There are cases in which one congregation has invited another to share a building owned by them, and they have together become a federated congregation though the property deed belongs to only one entity. These congregations have had to live out their ecumenical vocation in ways that give priority to their theological identity as the baptized and not in terms of constitutional boilerplate or real property law. The hospitality each offers the other is always reflective, that is, it invites me to consider the gifts the other brings me that may challenge and reshape my own identity, while being willing to share mine

---

20. Susan Durber, "Loving the Stranger," in Gibaut, *Called to Be*, 202–3.

with my partner at the risk they will be questioned or even rejected. Hospitality means the strength to welcome and to be vulnerable simultaneously to what the host and guest bring to one another.

Just as when a couple moves in together, two or more traditions bring their own baggage, both physical, dispositional, and imagined. One tradition might prefer chancel furnishings of a certain design, while for another such matters might be pure adiaphora. Two churches merging under one roof might bring furniture, beloved and evocative of their own past but badly mismatched when all put together in the same room. In Albany, Georgia, when St. Patrick's Episcopal invited the Lutheran Church of Our Savior to share their building, the Lutherans brought many of their furnishings, some of which were harmoniously incorporated into the Episcopal space, so that the church has two processional crosses, two sets of clergy chairs, and two baptismal fonts. The stone font from Our Savior was rededicated in a ceremony presided over by both bishops and placed in an outdoor worship center on the property. Nativity Holy Comforter Lutheran-Episcopal in Baltimore moved into common space. Rev. Stewart Lucas, the Episcopal rector, amused, noted that the combination of both sacristies created a surplus of purificators for communion. "How many purificators does one place need?" he quipped.[21]

North American weddings often include the "unity candle" ritual, where two candles, lit before the vows, are used to light one candle between them following the vows. Do the two then blow out their candles? The common wisdom has been to advise couples not to, since their respective selves are continuing entities that do not cease to be selves with boundaries by virtue of the marriage. Between the two, there is a new reality of communion that is only possible so long as the two remain two, each with their own "I" that is beloved by the other. The "one flesh" metaphor was never meant literally (it would make little sense) but allegorically, a "one flesh" of communion, mutual accountability, and space within each to find the other. As Volf puts it:

> The human self is formed not through a simple rejection of the other—through a binary logic of opposition and negation—but through a complex process of "taking in" and "keeping out." We are who we are not because we are separate from the others who are next to us, but because we are both separate and connected, both distinct and related; the boundaries that mark our identities are both barriers and bridges. . . . Identity is a result of the other; it arises out of the complex history of "differentiation" in which both

---

21. Thompson, "Blending Episcopal-Lutheran Congregations."

self and other take part by negotiating their identities in interaction with one another.[22]

When one I/self/group makes space for another, the roof is raised. Now the self lives in shared space, under a common roof. The one, while still fully itself, dies to that self. Boundary indicators are relativized and de-centered, as common space for both or more opens up around them and within them. I cannot know myself, even be myself, without the other. This is at the heart of the ecumenically shared mission of mutual discovery. Many participants in these churches report that they became better members of their own traditions by living in proximity to members of the other.

It is just the mission—under one roof—that is the dare. There may be quarrels under the roof, and the gift of diversity can sometimes be a burden. There are complications around budget, deeds, constitutions, worship, and judicatory relations, to name a few. On the one hand, some may long to reinforce the walls, or to erase all difference so that there is no "other" to bless or be blessed by, on the other. Not only are there differences to be expected among one constituency, but, in a multi-denominational congregation, there are two or more such collections of diversity. Whatever the case, "grace is gamble, always."[23] Where there is grace, there is inclusion, and inclusion always involves risk for both partners. It is just this risk, this dare, that is involved in *koinonia* of any sort, as Paul's Corinthians attest.

Buildings can be confining, though. And so can the traditions that inhabit them. The truth about buildings and traditions is that they are both in "motion"; buildings get remodeled, expanded, torn down and replaced, and traditions are dynamic, living realities, introducing new music, forms of speech and practices, while rethinking and re-presenting older ways of thinking and practicing the faith. Multi-denominational congregations should reflect on how their shared spaces might represent not just an aggregation of markers for their respective traditions—symbols of mutual hospitality to the other—but how those spaces might change over time to represent deeper unity or reassertion of individuality in ways that do no violence to the foundational hospitality.

SAFE OR BRAVE?

Much has been said lately about creating "safe space" for important discussions about identity, controversial ideas, or matters that might otherwise be

22. Volf, *After Our Likeness*, 66.
23. Smedes, *Forgive and Forget*, 137.

spoken of only with trusted confidants. A "safe space" is one in which one should presumably feel safe discussing sensitive topics. Educators have defined safe space as controlled space, an "environment in which everyone feels comfortable expressing themselves and participating fully, without fear of attack, ridicule, or denial of experience."[24] Perhaps the original "safe space" was the confessional booth in Catholic churches, where any and all sins were to be disclosed under the seal of priestly confidentiality. There was no divulging of even the worst sins. Safe space is a refuge from a world of judgment, space permissive for trying out new ideas or working through complex issues.

Can one be honest and "safe" at the same time? And, whose definition of safety gets privileged? Should not risk, controversy, and difficulty be expected, given that they cannot long be discussed in the abstract amongst flesh and blood human beings who occupy social spaces in differing ways? What might be instructive about these questions for ecumenical shared ministries?

Most social relationships generate conflict as they bring together people with unique histories, habits, and hopes. An ecumenical shared ministry is sometimes a bit like a marriage. Some are rocky, others smooth, and a few cannot survive. As in marriage and other difficult ways humans gather, a multi-denominational congregation is a commitment to journey through time together, committed to mutual fidelity and growth. Such mutual commitments—or what Dietrich Bonhoeffer described as "life together"—make inevitable difficult conversations and honest conflicts. This is why shared ministries must not only be "safe," but "brave."

Part of why bravery is required is that congregations are not static entities but stories in progress. People come and go from congregations, which, as Stanley Hauerwas points out, changes the congregational narrative.[25] The appearance of the "Other" can be a threat as much as an opportunity. The story changes with the coming of an outsider. And so, a new member joins a congregation and brings a wealth of experience in youth ministry, reviving a languishing youth program. Or, a same-sex couple join a congregation of an "open and affirming" denomination that, up until then, has only experienced ecclesial debates on inclusion in the abstract. Their congregational story is changed. To be missional and invitational is to risk constantly changing the shape of a congregation that may bring great gain or great discomfort. Combining two or more ecclesial stories involves just this risk, but on an even larger scale, as congregations, buildings, budgets, stories, and theologies come together.

24. Brian Arao and Kristi Clemens, "From Safe Spaces to Brave Spaces: A New Way to Frame Dialogue Around Diversity and Social Justice," in Landreman, *Art of Effective Facilitation*, 138.

25. Hauerwas, *Community of Character*, 22–23.

THE ECUMENICAL BODY OF CHRIST

"Ecumenism is far down my list of priorities," quipped a bishop with whom one of the authors ate lunch one day. Evangelism, church planting, and missions ranked near the top of this prelate's "to do" list, not unlike those of many church leaders. Sadly, this is a story often repeated: ecumenism is a low priority, as though it were some sort of impractical delicacy. Maybe it can be enjoyed if time and resources permit. Or, it seems ecumenism lacks sufficient "muscularity," and is thus not mandated by denominations gasping for sustainability, even survival, in coming decades. Only what is tested and proven gets funded. This tendency not to prioritize unity may also reflect an unconsciously held hermeneutic when reading the gospels. Jesus may have *prayed* for unity (John 17:21), but he *mandated* evangelism and mission (Matt 28:19). Is a bias toward fulfilling command and away from long-term practice (e.g., prayer) at play here, what ethicists might distinguish as a rule-based versus a practice-based ethic?

A theological judgment is being made on the part of those who would de-center the church's quest for unity. A certain ecclesiology is being presupposed that privileges expedience by bifurcating mission and unity. Could this be a faulty ecclesiology, of which no one less than Jesus, who prayed for unity, and Paul, who illustrated it in some of his letters, would not approve?

We have spoken of walls and roofs, but what of foundations? Consider the all-or-nothing call Jesus issued to his disciples to "follow me." Not only was the economic basis of their lives (mostly fishing) suddenly put on hold, but more existentially, their self-understanding and their presumably settled relationship to God were about to be risked. With every healing witnessed and parable heard, their sense of self and God was being de-centered. The "old self" to which they would be asked to die was gradually being ripped up, off set, and cast away in favor of uncompromising discipleship. They could come to live what Paul later gave voice to, saying: "We know that our old self was crucified with him so that the body of sin might be destroyed, and we might no longer be enslaved to sin. For whoever has died is freed from sin. But if we have died with Christ, we believe that we will also live with him" (Rom 6:6–8; cf. Eph 2:15; 4:22–24; Col 3:9–11). As surely as the sin of division is among those former enslavements destroyed in Christ's rising, so is unity's source the new creation in Christ created by his wounds and sealed by his rising, making, as the Colossians verses cited above suggest, one out of two.

As this chapter has shown, what makes multi-denominational parish ecclesiology different from "siloed" single-denomination churches is that multi-denominational congregations exist because historic fissures have occasioned their possibility. To borrow Volf's language, mutual exclusion makes possible mutual embrace. They exist also to make space for the other, and, in so doing, they offer a sign of the otherness-in-communion implicit in creation and made explicit in the New Creation of the risen Christ. While in a certain sense this is universally true of all ecclesial gatherings, this is acutely true of multi-denominational congregations because they are spaces intentionally made for mutual accommodation across traditional boundaries. All congregations to a certain extent may welcome the stranger, or the other, in general, by whatever markers the other is identified. Single-denomination churches are usually proud to boast attendees, spouses of members, etc., who come from other denominations. The other in shared ministries is the other tradition—or two—that inhabit the same space. So, while embracing difference is part and parcel of all Christian catholicity, multi-denominational congregations are local assemblies gathered specifically to witness to the unity found despite disparate denominational identities. And this witness always involves a risk, a dare.

CRUCIFORM ECCLESIAL EXISTENCE

There is a "[g]racious emptiness at the heart of creation."[26] It is God's hospitable space-time continuum for the dazzling multiplicity of beings, from galaxies to gnats. This is the space-time where humans live, move, and have their being, our imaginations and desires. It is also that which humans have exploited in violence, greed, and the infliction of untold suffering upon others. And it is also that into which Jesus has come, nailed to the cross, signifying that God will not be God without humanity.

The risk Jesus took in going to the cross was a risk of everlasting death—to all appearances, the sure and certain end to his life, his ministry, and his legacy. As John's gospel narrates, Jesus' parting command to Mary and the beloved disciple at the foot of the cross was to look after one another (John 19:26–27). A venerable interpretation sees the nascent church in this community formed at the cross. The community of Mary and the disciple, of each to other, was not only born at the cross, but shaped by the cross itself, as self-giving love poured out by God to God's certain other, the world.

Jesus' death—a finite thing—opened up the infinity of eternal, risen life. Gracious emptiness was made in Jesus' wounds for life's ultimate otherness in death. And, within the space of the wounds, the space of absence, was the space for the church itself, the *koinonia* of believers in the death of Christ (Rom 6:3–11). The wounds create space inside of which the church may live.[27]

26. Bauerschmidt, "Wounds of Christ," 87.

27. Bauerschmidt, "Wounds of Christ," 85.

There is a dare, a risk, in the *kenosis*, the self-emptying of Christ. An ecclesiology based on a dare is inherently Christological, as it calls for mutual self-emptying. But, haven't we argued that the self does not cease when in communion with the other? How does this self-emptying happen? The emptiness that is the cross was not, after all, the absence of Christ, but his very presence there. His whole ministry was epitomized in the crucifixion, present in self-offering for the sake of the world, yet fully himself. And so it goes with his ecumenical body, the church, springing forth from that sacrifice. The church can be called a mystical body in which that sacrifice is continually made present as members of the body love one another by offering—being—Christ to one another, and together, being Christ to the world, even as his broken and yet reconciled body, awaiting with hope the fullness of unity as those who live in the power of the resurrection.

The wounds create gracious space in which creation is re-created. God negates Godself, in love, for the world and its multiplicity, so that it may find its unity in Christ, in his wounds. Wounds, though, are not passive emptiness that can be filled with otherness. They gush forth blood, too. The very life they metaphorically make room for becomes a wellspring of life.[28] It is through the cross that space is made for the church, and it is in those wounds that the inherently ecumenical body of the church, is born and nurtured.

> With a kindly countenance our good Lord looked into his side, and he gazed with joy, and with his sweet regard he drew his creature's understanding into his side by the same wound; and there he revealed a fair and delectable place, large enough for all humankind that will be saved and will rest in peace and love. And with that he brought to mind the dear and precious blood and water which he suffered to be shed for love. And in this sweet sight he showed his blessed heart split in two, and as he rejoiced he showed my understanding a part of his blessed divinity, as much as was his will at that time, strengthening my poor soul to understand what can be said, that is the endless love which was without beginning and is and always shall be.[29]
>
> —Julian of Norwich

---

28. Bauerschmidt, "Wounds of Christ," 84, 85.
29. Julian, *Showings*, 220.

Bibliography

WORKS CITED

Anglican-Reformed International Commission. *God's Reign and Our Unity: Report of the Anglican-Reformed International Commission, 1981–1984: Woking, England, 1984*. Edinburgh: Saint Andrew Press, 1984.

Barker, G. Harvie, ed. *A Lively Option: Voices from Shared Ministry Congregations*. Penticton, BC: British Columbia Conference, United Church of Canada, 1994.

Bauerschmidt, Frederick C. "The Wounds of Christ." *Journal of Literature & Theology* 5:1 (March 1991) 83–100.

Billings, Taylor. *Multiply-Affiliated Congregations in the United Church of Christ. A Research Report of the UCC Center for Analytics, Research and Data (CARD)*. Cleveland: United Church of Christ, 2015.

Blumberg, Antonia. "The 30 Least Religious Cities in the United States: Portland Tops the List." HuffPost, US Edition, August 8, 2015. http://www.huffingtonpost.com/entry/most-religiously-unaffiliated-us-cities_us_55c52ac3e4b0f1cbf1e526b0.

Boff, Leonardo. *Holy Trinity, Perfect Community*. Maryknoll, NY: Orbis, 2000.

Braaten, Carl E., and Robert W. Jensen. *In One Body Through the Cross: The Princeton Proposal for Christian Unity: A Call to the Churches from an Ecumenical Study Group*. Grand Rapids, MI: Eerdmans, 2003.

Campbell, J. Y. "KOINONIA and Its Cognates in the New Testament." *Journal of Biblical Literature* 51 (1932) 352–80.

Church of the Holy Apostles. *The First Ten Years*. Virginia Beach: n.d.

Church of the Holy Apostles. *Parish Profile*. Virginia Beach: April 1991.

The Church: Towards a Common Vision. Faith and Order Paper No. 214. Geneva: World Council of Churches, 2013.

Cohen, Richard, ed. *Face to Face with Levinas*. Albany: State University of New York Press, 1986.

Ecumenical Shared Ministries Handbook. Ecumenical Shared Ministries Task Force, 2011. http://www.united-church.ca/sites/default/files/handbook_ecumenical-shared-ministries.pdf.

Einstein, Mara. *Brands of Faith: Marketing Religion in a Commercial Age*. Abingdon, UK: Routledge, 2008.

The Episcopal Church. *The Book of Common Prayer and Administration of the Sacraments and Other Rites and Ceremonies of the Church: Together with the Psalter or Psalms of David According to the Use of the Episcopal Church.* New York: Seabury, 1979.

———. "Full Communion Partners." http://www.episcopalchurch.org/page/full-communion-partners.

Evangelical Lutheran Church in America. *Ecumenism: The Vision of the Evangelical Lutheran Church in America.* Chicago: ELCA, 1991.

Fennell, Austin. "Rev. McKillop's Diary." *Alberta Northwest Conference United Church of Canada Historical Society Journal* 24 (May 2011) 39–41.

Ferguson, Michael. "Shared Congregation Project." YouTube, July 10, 2013. https://www.youtube.com/watch?v=qo12TUjwxJ8.

Ferguson, Michael B., and James E. Parke. "Celebrating Together." *The Living Church* 243 (August 28, 2011) 27.

Flannery, Austin. *Vatican Council II.* Collegeville, MN: Liturgical, 1996.

Ford, John T., and Darlis J. Swan. *Twelve Tales Untold: A Study Guide for Ecumenical Reception.* Grand Rapids, MI: Eerdmans, 1993.

Friedman, Thomas L. *Thank You for Being Late: An Optimist's Guide to Thriving in an Age of Acceleration.* New York: Farrar, Straus, & Giroux, 2016.

Gardner, Matt. "Congregational Development: On the Rediscovery of Anglican Identity." Anglican Church of Canada, September 20, 2016. http://www.anglican.ca/news/congregational-development.

Gibaut, John, ed. *Called to Be the One Church: Faith and Order at Crete.* Geneva: World Council of Churches, 2012.

Glatfelter, Charles Henry. *Pastors and People: German Lutheran and Reformed Churches in the Pennsylvania Field, 1717–1783.* Breinigsville, PA: Pennsylvania German Society, 1981.

González, Justo L. *The History of Theological Education.* Nashville: Abingdon, 2015.

Gunton, Colin. *The Promise of Trinitarian Theology.* Edinburgh: T&T Clark, 1993.

Harrison, Nonna Verna. "Zizioulas on Communion and Otherness." *St. Vladimir's Theological Quarterly* 42:3–4 (1998) 278–300.

Hauerwas, Stanley. *A Community of Character: Toward a Constructive Christian Social Ethic.* Notre Dame: University of Notre Dame Press, 1981.

A History of the Commission on the Welfare of the Union Church with Statements Prepared and Adopted by It. [S.l.]: Commission on the Welfare of the Union Church, 1961.

Ingle-Gillis, William C. *The Trinity and Ecumenical Church Thought: The Church-Event.* Aldershot, England: Ashgate, 2007.

Julian, of Norwich. *Showings.* New York: Paulist, 1978.

Kärkkäinen, Veli-Matti. *Introduction to Ecclesiology: Ecumenical, Historical and Global Perspectives.* Downers Grove, IL: InterVarsity, 2002.

Kavanagh, Aidan. *Liturgical Theology.* New York: Pueblo, 1984.

Kinnamon, Michael. *Can a Renewal Movement Be Renewed? Questions for the Future of Ecumenism.* Grand Rapids, MI: Eerdmans, 2014.

———. *Truth and Community: Diversity and Its Limits in the Ecumenical Movement.* Grand Rapids: Eerdmans, 1988.

Klein, Naomi. *No Logo: Taking Aim at the Brand Bullies.* Toronto: Vintage Canada, 2000.

Landreman, Lisa M. *The Art of Effective Facilitation: Reflections from Social Justice Educators.* Sterling, VA: Stylus, 2013.

Levinas, Emmanuel. *Totality and Infinity: An Essay on Exteriority.* Pittsburgh: Duquesne University Press, 1969.

Long, Paul. *Indian Hill Church Blue Book History.* Cincinnati: n.d.

Longenecker, Stephen L. *Piety and Tolerance: Pennsylvania German Religion, 1700–1850.* Pietist and Wesleyan Studies 6. Metuchen, NJ: Scarecrow, 1994.

Macauley, Howard K. "A Social and Intellectual History of Elementary Education in Pennsylvania to 1850." PhD diss., University of Pennsylvania, 1972.

Madden, Raymond. *Being Ethnographic: A Guide to the Theory and Practice of Ethnography.* London: SAGE, 2010.

Marcel, Gabriel. *The Mystery of Being.* 2 vols. Chicago: H. Regnery, 1950.

Martin, Dale. B. *The Corinthian Body.* New Haven: Yale University Press, 1995.

Merritt, Anne. "Why Learn a Foreign Language? Benefits of Bilingualism." *The Telegraph,* June 19, 2013. http://www.telegraph.co.uk/education/educationopinion/10126883/ Why-learn-a-foreign-language-Benefits-of-bilingualism.html.

Moschella, Mary Clark. *Ethnography as a Pastoral Practice: An Introduction.* Cleveland, OH: Pilgrim, 2008.

Nelson, E. Clifford, ed. *The Lutherans in North America.* Philadelphia: Fortress, 1980.

Nelson, Michael Lee. "Living into Unity: A Proposal for a Roman Catholic/United Methodist Ecumenical Parish." DMin Thesis, Wesley Theological Seminary, 2006.

Neufeld, Thomas R. Yoder. "Koinonia: The Gift We Hold Together." *Mennonite Quarterly Review* 86:3 (July 2012) 339–52.

Nolt, Steven M. *Foreigners in Their Own Land: Pennsylvania Germans in the Early Republic.* University Park: Pennsylvania State University Press, 2008.

O'Gara, Margaret. *The Ecumenical Gift Exchange.* Collegeville, MN: Liturgical, 1998.

Pelikan, Jaroslav, and Valerie R. Hotchkiss. *Creeds & Confessions of Faith in the Christian Tradition.* New Haven: Yale University Press, 2003.

Pontifical Council for Promoting Christian Unity. *Directory for the Application of Principles and Norms on Ecumenism.* Vatican City, 1993.

Ratzlaff, Vern, Ursula Wiig, Carol Pek, and Merle McGowan, eds. *God's Reconciling Grace: Prairie Centre for Ecumenism 25 years of Ecumenical Leadership, 1984–2009.* Saskatoon, Saskatchewan: Prairie Centre for Ecumenism, 2009.

"Religion: Two Altars, One Mass." *Time,* February 2, 1981. http://content.time.com/time/ magazine/article/0,9171,920979,00.html.

Roof, Wade Clark. *Spiritual Marketplace: Baby Boomers and the Remaking of American Religion.* Princeton: Princeton University Press, 1999.

Rush, Benjamin. *An Account of the Manners of the German Inhabitants of Pennsylvania.* Lancaster: Pennsylvania-German Society, 1910.

Saarinen, Martin F. *The Life Cycle of a Congregation.* Washington, DC: Alban Institute, 1986.

Saliers, Don, and Emily Saliers. *A Song to Sing, a Life to Live: Reflections on Music as Spiritual Practice.* San Francisco: Jossey-Bass, 2005.

Salmon, Ann. "The Effect of Worship on Ecumenical Shared Ministries that Are Lutheran, Anglican and/or United Church of Canada." DMin Project Report, Saskatoon Theological Union, 2017.

Schuth, Katarina. *Seminary Formation: Recent History, Current Circumstances, New Directions.* Collegeville, MN: Liturgical, 2016.

Small, Joseph D. "Ecclesial Identity and Ecumenical Decisions in the Presbyterian Church (U.S.A.)." *Journal of Ecumenical Studies* 37:1 (Winter 2000) 1–12.

Smedes, Lewis B. *Forgive and Forget: Healing the Hurts We Don't Deserve*. San Francisco: Harper and Row, 1984.

Thiessen, Gesa Elsbeth, ed. *Ecumenical Ecclesiology: Unity, Diversity, and Otherness in a Fragmented World*. London: T&T Clark, 2011.

Thompson, Richelle. "Blending Episcopal-Lutheran Congregations in Baltimore." *Episcopal News Service*, Dec. 13, 2016. https://www.episcopalchurch.org/library/article/blending-episcopal-lutheran-congregations-baltimore.

———. "*Called to Common Mission*: 15 years of Episcopal-Lutheran Partnership." *Episcopal News Service*, Dec. 12., 2016. https://www.episcopalchurch.org/library/article/called-common-mission-15-years-episcopal-lutheran-partnership.

Twitchell, James B. *Branded Nation: The Marketing of Megachurch, College Inc., and Museumworld*. New York: Simon and Schuster, 2004.

Usunier, Jean-Claude, and Jörg Stolz, eds. *Religions as Brands: New Perspectives on the Marketization of Religion and Spirituality*. Burlington, VT: Ashgate, 2014.

Veling, Terry A. "'For You Alone': A Reading of Transcendence and Relationship in Emannuel Levinas." *Australian eJournal of Australia* 14 (2009) 1–14. http://www.academia.edu/229702/_For_You_Alone_-_Transcendence_and_Relationship_in_Levinas_Writings.

Volf, Miroslav. *After Our Likeness: The Church As the Image of the Trinity*. Grand Rapids: Eerdmans, 1998.

———. *Exclusion and Embrace: A Theological Exploration of Identity, Otherness, and Reconciliation*. Nashville, TN: Abingdon, 2008.

Xiao, Na, and Fang Wan. "Co-Branding with an Emotional Brand: Identity Threat and Coping Strategies among Loyal Consumers." *Advances in Consumer Research* 38 (2011) 901–3.

Zikmund, Barbara Brown, ed. *Hidden Histories in the United Church of Christ*. New York: United Church Press, 1987.

Zizioulas, John. *Being As Communion: Studies in Personhood and the Church*. Crestwood, NY: St. Vladimir's Seminary Press, 1985.

INTERVIEWS BY AUTHORS

All Saints in Big Sky, a Shared Ministry of the Episcopal and Lutheran (ELCA) Churches, Big Sky, Montana

The Rev. Miriam A. E. Schmidt. Interview by Mitzi J. Budde, October 29, 2015.

Brandermill Community Church, Midlothian, Virginia

Angela Branyon, Jeff Branyon, Myra Branyon, the Rev. Ed Kross, Barbara Larson, Victor Larson, Dr. Harry A. Raddin, Jr., Margaret Raddin. Group interview by William McDonald, July 19, 2015.

Broadway Disciples United Church, Winnipeg, Manitoba

The Rev. Ray Cuthbert. Interview by Sandra Beardsall, July 15, 2012.
Awit Marcelino. Interview by Sandra Beardsall, July 16, 2012.

The Church of the Holy Apostles Episcopal-Roman Catholic Parish, Virginia Beach, Virginia

Darden Dickerson, Jack Dickerson, Joan Flowers, Jean Koch, Carolyn Pollie, Ben Russo, Bonnie Startt, Lee Startt. Lay group interview by Mitzi J. Budde, November 1, 2015.
The Rev. Michael Ferguson and the Rev. Gary Harmeyer. Clergy interview by Mitzi J. Budde, November 1, 2015.

The Church of the Nativity and Holy Comforter, Baltimore, Maryland

The Rev. Stewart Lucas. Interviews by Mitzi J. Budde, May 12, 2015 and November 6, 2015.
The Rev. Stewart Lucas. Interview with the Lutheran Episcopal Coordinating Committee of the Metropolitan Washington, DC Synod, Diocese of Washington and Diocese of Virginia, May 23, 2016.
The Rev. Stewart Lucas. Interview with the National Lutheran Episcopal Coordinating Committee, May 10, 2016.
Jeff Valentine. Interview with the Lutheran Episcopal Coordinating Committee of the Metropolitan Washington, DC Synod, Diocese of Washington and Diocese of Virginia, May 23, 2016.

Community Church at Tellico Village, Loudon, Tennessee

The Rev. Devin Phillips. Interview by William McDonald, August 9, 2017.

Deer Park United Church and Calvin Presbyterian Church, Toronto, Ontario

The Rev. Marie Goodyear. Interview by Sandra Beardsall, June 5, 2012.

Epiphany Lutheran and Episcopal Church, Marina, California

The Rev. Jon Perez. Interview by Mitzi J. Budde, May 10, 2016.

First Federated Church, North Jackson, Ohio

The Rev. Jack Acri. Interview by William McDonald, June 15, 2015.

Anne Acri, Joan Acri, Shaun Andrews, Betty J. Byram, Mary Himes, James Lawrence, Pam Lawrence, Mary Sue McKinney, Joyce Slusarczyk. Group interview by William McDonald, June 15, 2015.

Holy Faith Church, Saline, Michigan

The Rev. Ian Reed Twiss. Interview with Lutheran Episcopal Coordinating Committee, November 6, 2014.

Huff's Union Church, Hereford Township, Pennsylvania

Carl Arner, Minerva Arner, Joanne Benfield, Marvin Diehl, Kay Kriebel, the Rev. Jane Kropa, Gary L. Moll. Group interview by William McDonald, May 31, 2015.

The Rev. Jane Kropa, Huff's Union Church; the Rev. Jerel Gade, St. Peter's Union Church, Macungie, PA; the Rev. Homer E. Royer, Jerusalem Western Salisbury Church, Allentown, PA. Clergy group interview by William P. McDonald, June 1, 2015.

Indian Hill Church, Cincinnati, Ohio

The Rev. Stephen Caine, the Rev. Heather Buchanan Wiseman. Interview by William McDonald, June 14, 2015.

Lamb of God Church: A Lutheran Episcopal Congregation, Fort Myers, Florida

Cheryl Frogge, Judith Frye, David Johnson, Susan Nicoletti, Judith Olson, Chris Perna, Thomas Rutkowski, Gina Sadri, Maureen Vath, Glenn Whitehouse, Elena Wild. Board of Trustees group conversation with Mitzi J. Budde, March 20, 2016.

The Rev. Walter Fohs. Conversation with the National Lutheran Episcopal Coordinating Committee via WebEx, October 20, 2011.

The Rev. Dr. James Reho. Interview by Mitzi J. Budde, March 21, 2016.

Spirit of Grace, formerly Asbury Our Redeemer Partnership, Hood River, Oregon

Linda Boris, Deborah Chenoweth, the Rev. David King, Melissa Mimier, the Rev. Judith Ann Richards, Gigi Siekkinen. Clergy and lay group interview by Mitzi J. Budde, August 2, 2015.

Spirit of Grace at Mission of the Atonement, an Inclusive Community of Lutherans and Catholics, Beaverton, Oregon

John Buesseler, the Rev. Laurie Larson Caesar, Nick Cannard, Valerie Cannard, Rachel Miller, Burt Parcher, Christopher Predeek, Barbara Smith, Neal Stixrud, M. Kathleen Truman. Clergy and laity group interview by Mitzi J. Budde, August 9, 2015.

Spirit of Grace, West Bloomfield, Michigan

The Rev. Stephen Bancroft, Joyce Campbell, Susan Fine, Susan Ludwiczak, Geoffrey Newcomb, Janet Timmons, Wilma White, Jim Van Blarcum. Clergy and laity group interview by Mitzi J. Budde, August 23, 2015.
The Rev. Mary Duerksen. Interview by Mitzi J. Budde, August 23, 2015.
The Rev. Manisha Dostert. Presentation to Lutheran Episcopal Coordinating Committee, November 6, 2014.
James Bugg, Louise Bugg. Outreach Group interview by Mitzi J. Budde, August 23, 2015.

St. Peter's Ecumenical Church, Slave Lake, Alberta

Debbie Anderson. Interview by Sandra Beardsall, September 10, 2011.
Janice Nowochin. Interview by Sandra Beardsall, September 12, 2011.
François Prévost. Interview by Sandra Beardsall, September 10, 2011.
Marge Procyshyn. Interview by Sandra Beardsall, September 12, 2011.
The Rev. Leigh Sinclair. Interview by Sandra Beardsall, September 12, 2011.
Several interviewees' names are withheld by mutual consent, September 10–12, 2011.

Sunriver Christian Fellowship, Sunriver, Oregon

Doris Brannan, Chris Hamilton, Karen Newcomb, Doug Vakoc, Bob Vogel. Board members interview by Mitzi J. Budde, August 5, 2015.
James Adams, Gene Bennington, Jane Boubel, Jenny Long, Ellie Luba, Linda Porter. Lay group interview by Mitzi J. Budde, August 5, 2015.
The Rev. Nancy Sargent McGrath-Green. Interview by Mitzi J. Budde, August 5, 2015.
The Rev. Nancy Sargent McGrath-Green. National Lutheran Episcopal Coordinating Committee, Chicago, February 9, 2017.
The Rev. Robert Pearson. Interview by Mitzi J. Budde, August 5, 2015.
The Rev. Frank Brocker, the Rev. Charles Christopher, the Rev. John Nesby, the Rev. Jack Kiekel. Retired clergy group interview by Mitzi J. Budde, August 5, 2015.

Trinity Ecumenical Parish, Smith Mountain Lake, Virginia

The Rev. Philip Bouknight, Rich Cairns, Connie Canova, Fred Canova, Christine Collins, Lorraine Conary, Mary H. Epting, Lois E. Garlough, Kathleen Greenan, Daniel L.

Jones, Nancy Jones, Chuck Koyanagi, Penny Larsen, Kevin Leap, Pidge Morgan, David R. Phelps, Wheat Wallenborn. Clergy and lay group interview by William McDonald, July 18, 2015.

United Christian Parish, Reston, Virginia

The Rev. Joan Bell-Haynes. Interview by Mitzi J. Budde, June 29, 2015.
Mary Jackson, Fran McElvey, Lois McMahon, Kathleen Schauer-Schmidt. Lay group interview by Mitzi J. Budde, June 29, 2015.
The Rev. D. Jay Losher. Interview by Mitzi J. Budde, June 29, 2015.
The Rev. Kay Rodgers. Interview by Mitzi J. Budde, August 21, 2015.

Windermere Valley Shared Ministry, Invermere, British Columbia

Laura Hermakin. Interview by Sandra Beardsall, April 2015.

Other Interviews

The Rev. Claire Burkat, ELCA Bishop of the Southeastern Pennsylvania Synod, Lutheran Episcopal Coordinating Committee meeting, Chicago, September 9, 2015.
The Most Rev. Remi De Roo. Interview by Sandra Beardsall, Saskatoon, Saskatchewan, October 11, 2012.

ARCHIVES

Clare A. Holmes. Interview for "Heritage Alive Program," June 13, 1977, transcribed. Acc #2006—EX; Box 1920; file 10. United Church of Canada British Columbia Conference Archives, Vancouver.
Kamloops Okanagan Presbytery Minutes, 1981. 2006 EX, Box 546/4. United Church of Canada, British Columbia Conference Archives, Vancouver.
Kootenay Presbytery Minutes, 2006 EX, Box 534. United Church of Canada, British Columbia Conference Archives, Vancouver.
Stephen P. Kristenson, Bishop. "To the Congregations of the Synod of AB and the Territories," Nov. 28, 1997. Acc. #2008.061C—Box 1–9 Ecumenical Shared Ministries (1996–2001). United Church of Canada Archives, Toronto.
St. Paul's-St. Cuthbert's Church, Princeton, BC, Annual Report. PRN SP Box 3; file 31— Annual Reports, United Church of Canada, British Columbia Conference Archives, Vancouver.

CHURCH CONSTITUTIONS, COVENANTS, AND AGREEMENTS

Agreement Between the Reformed and Lutheran Congregations Worshipping in the Peaked Mountain Church, Rockingham Co., Va., October 31, 1769. Record of the Peaked Mountain Church. Virginia Vital Records. Supplied to the authors by Christopher Agnew.

Bylaws of Spirit of Grace Church, Sylvan Lake.

Bylaws of Spirit of Grace Church (A Lutheran and Episcopal Community), West Bloomfield, Michigan, 2015.

Churches Together in England, "Model Governing Document for Single Congregation Local Ecumenical Partnerships." Revised 2013. http://www.cte.org.uk/Groups/234952/Home/Resources/Local_Ecumenical_Partnerships/Single_Congregation_LEPs/Model_Governing_Document/Model_Governing_Document.aspx.

Constitution and By-Laws for Asbury Our Redeemer Partnership, a cooperative church of the Evangelical Lutheran Church in America and the United Methodist Church. December 2015.

The Constitution of the Anglican/Roman Catholic Church of the Holy Apostles, Richmond, Virginia. 1978. Amended 2012.

Constitution of the United Christian Parish of Reston, Virginia. 2003. Revised 2004.

Covenant Agreement and By-Laws, Sunriver Christian Fellowship, Inc. 2003.

A Covenant for Ministry between Trinity Lutheran Church of Spiritwood and Bissell Memorial Church of Spiritwood. Spiritwood, Saskatchewan. April 2009.

The Episcopal Church and the Evangelical Lutheran Church in America. "Called to Common Mission." 2001. https://www.episcopalchurch.org/page/agreement-full-communion-called-common-mission.

———. The Orderly Exchange of Pastors and Priests under Called to Common Mission: Principles and Guidelines. 2001. http://arc.episcopalchurch.org/ministry/oepp/.

Evangelical Lutheran Church in America, "Documents of Governance and Policy Related to Federated and Union Congregations," November 14, 1999. http://download.elca.org/ELCA%20Resource%20Repository/Goverance_Docs_Federated_Union_Congregations_Nov_99.pdf?_ga=2.189047467.1488100953.1501775872-1734677353.1501775872.

Evangelical Lutheran Church in America, the Presbyterian Church (USA), the Reformed Church in America, and the United Church of Christ, A Formula of Agreement (1997). https://www.pcusa.org/resource/ecumenical-formula-agreement/.

"FAQs about the Nativity-Holy Comforter Joint Ministry." Unpublished handout from the Rev. Stewart Lucas and the Rev. David Eisenhuth to the national Lutheran Episcopal Coordinating Committee, May 10, 2016.

Joint Anglican Lutheran Commission, "Guidelines for Collaborative Congregational Ministries for Lutherans and Anglicans in Canada." Vancouver, BC, 2006. http://www.elcic.ca/Documents/documents/2006-GuidelinesforCollaborativeMinistry.pdf.

Memorandum of Agreement, the Diocese of Eastern Newfoundland and Labrador and the Newfoundland Conference of the United Church of Canada, Humber Presbytery. Re: Joint Ministry, St. Mark's Congregation, Churchill Falls, Labrador. April 1978.

Memorandum of Understanding of the Lutheran Church of the Holy Comforter and the Episcopal Church of the Nativity, Cedarcroft. Nov. 15, 2015.

National Convention of the Evangelical Lutheran Church in Canada and the General Synod of the Anglican Church of Canada, "Called to Full Communion (The Waterloo Declaration)," 2001.

WEBSITES CITED

Christ Church Gabriola, British Columbia. http://www.gabriolaunitedchurch.ca/.

Church of the Holy Apostles, Virginia Beach, Virginia. http://www.holyapostlesvb.org.

Community Church at Tellico Village, Tennessee. https://www.tellicochurch.com.

Episcopal Shared Ministry Asset Map. https://ccm.episcopalassetmap.org.

Huff's Union Church, Alburtis, Pennsylvania. http://www.huffschurch.com.

Indian Hill Church, Cincinnati, Ohio. "Our History." http://www.indianhillchurch.org/our-history.

Prairie Centre for Ecumenism, Ecumenical Shared Ministries Directory. http://pcecumenism.ca/esm.

Spirit of Grace at Mission of the Atonement, an Inclusive Community of Lutherans and Catholics, Beaverton, Oregon. http://www.motaspirit.org.

Trinity Ecumenical Parish, Smith Mountain Lake, Virginia. http://trinityecumenical.dioswva.org/.

US Census Bureau Fact Finder. http://factfinder.census.gov.

Made in the USA
Middletown, DE
23 January 2020